TWELVE
SONS OF
ISRAEL

TWELVE
SONS OF
ISRAEL

Dramatic accounts of twelve rabbis
who sought for the Messiah...
and found Him.

A Publication of the MJAA and the IAMCS

Published by
the *Messianic Jewish Alliance of America* and
the *International Alliance of Messianic Congregations and Synagogues*

www.mjaa.org
www.iamcs.org

Printed in Toronto, Ontario
Canada

All rights reserved © 2013
ISBN 978-0-9894669-0-5

Senior Editor
Messianic Rabbi Jeffrey Forman
IAMCS Chairman 2009-2013

This is a special abridged and updated edition of the book "Rabbis Meet Jesus the Messiah" published by Messianic Good News. It includes several additional accounts and the language has been updated using modern Messianic terminology.

Table of Contents

INTRODUCTION

Within these pages are the dramatic accounts of ten Orthodox and two Reform rabbis. These rabbis were highly educated and worked at length within the framework of traditional Judaism. Although they come from different countries and backgrounds, they testify with a unified voice that they earnestly sought for the Messiah...and found him.

Through careful consideration of the Jewish scriptures, these twelve rabbis made the startling discovery that Yeshua (Jesus) is the long awaited Messiah. These men, some obscure and some famous, faced diverse inward struggles over the truths they discovered. By believing and following Yeshua, they also experienced personal attacks from those near to them. Despite the resulting pain and loss, each remained deeply committed to Yeshua as the Messiah and deeply committed to the Jewish people.

We became aware of these biographies and autobiographies and were profoundly moved. Each account is stunning and unique. We chose these twelve accounts, like long-forgotten jewels, to update, polish and display. These are sons of our people—real rabbis who had real experiences. They belong to the history and heritage of the Jewish people. Their voices, though muted throughout the years, carry words that are clear and compelling for us today. These are stories that must be told and voices that must be heard.

RABBI LEOPOLD COHN

Born: Berezna, Hungary, 1862
Died: Brooklyn, NY, 1937
Smikha:1880

RABBI LEOPOLD COHN

Life began for Leopold Cohn in the little town of Berezna, in the eastern part of Hungary. At the age of seven a great calamity befell the young lad; he lost both of his parents in the same year and was left to fend, as well as he could, for himself. In later years, he often recalled how those days of terrible loneliness and bitter struggle for existence taught him to trust in God with all of his heart. It seems natural then, to find young Cohn, after his Bar Mitzvah, determined to enter upon a course of study with a view to becoming eventually a rabbi and leader among his people. That he gave good account of himself as a student we conclude from the fact that at the age of eighteen, he graduated from the Talmudic academies with a record of high scholarship and with commendations as a worthy teacher of the Law.

Following the completion of his formal studies and the subsequent receipt of "smikha" or ordination, Rabbi Cohn contracted a very happy marriage and, in keeping with the custom of the time, became installed in his wife's paternal home, there to devote himself to the further study of the sacred writings.[1]

A part of his morning devotions was the repetition of the twelfth article of the Jewish creed, which declares, "I believe with a perfect faith in the coming of the Messiah, and though He tarry, yet will I wait daily for His coming." The regular use of this affirmation of faith fanned to a flame the desire of his heart for the fulfillment of God's promises and the speedy restoration of scattered Israel.[2] "Why does the Messiah tarry? When will He come?" These were questions which continually agitated the young rabbi's mind.[3]

During my leisure, I had frequent recourse to my Talmud, in which I at one time read the following: *"The world is to stand six thousand years, vis., two thousand confusion and void, two thousand with the law, and two thousand the time of Messiah."*[4] Rashi, the very first and most authoritative commentator gives as an explanation on the last clause: "Because after the second two thousand years, the Messiah must have come and the wicked kingdom should have been destroyed." This greatly excited my attention. I was accustomed to sit on the ground almost every Thursday night at twelve o'clock, weeping, crying, and mourning for about an hour, over the destruction of Jerusalem (called by the Jews "Tickin Chazoss") and repeating the 137 Psalm.

---

[1] *Note.* From "When Jews Face Christ," edited by Dr. Henry Einspruch, 1939, 2nd ed., p. 144. Copyright 1939 by American Board of Missions to the Jews, Brooklyn.
[2] *Note.* From "When Jews Face Christ," edited by Dr. Henry Einspruch, 1939, 2nd ed., p. 145. Copyright 1939 by American Board of Missions to the Jews, Brooklyn.
[3] *Note.* From "When Jews Face Christ," edited by Dr. Henry Einspruch, 1939, 2nd ed., p. 146. Copyright 1939 by American Board of Missions to the Jews, Brooklyn.
[4] See Babylonian Talmud Tractate Sanhedrin 97a.

I was very anxiously awaiting the coming of our Messiah, and now I saw that his time was over two thousand years ago, according to the Jewish reckoning. I was surprised and asked myself, "Is it possible that the time which God had fixed for the appearance of our Messiah has passed away without the promise of our true and living God being fulfilled?" I never had any doubt of the truthfulness of the Talmud; I believed every part of it to be holy, but now I looked upon this passage as a simple legend.[5]

Rabbi Cohn decided to begin a study of the original predictions of the prophets. However, the very contemplation of the act filled him with fear, for, according to the teaching of the rabbis, "Cursed are the bones of him who calculates the time of the end."[6] And so it was that with trembling hands, expecting at any moment to be struck by a bolt from heaven, but with an irresistible eagerness, he opened the book of the Prophet Daniel and began to read.

From the twenty-fourth verse of the chapter before him (chapter nine), he deduced without difficulty that the coming of the Messiah should have taken place four hundred years after Daniel received the prophecy of the seventy weeks from the divine messenger. The scholar, accustomed to the intricate and often veiled polemical treatises of the Talmud, now found himself strangely captivated by the clear and soul-satisfying declarations of the Word of God. It was not long before he began to question

---

[5] *Note.* From "To an Ancient People: The Autobiography of Rabbi Leopold Cohn," by Rabbi Leopold Cohn, 1996, p. 6-7. Copyright 1996 by Chosen People Ministries. Reprinted with permission.
[6] See Babylonian Talmud Tractate Sanhedrin 97b.

in his mind the reliability of the Talmud, seeing that in matters so vital it differed from the Holy Scriptures. [7]

Without being fully conscious of it, Rabbi Cohn was travelling toward a parting of the ways. A crisis was inevitable and it broke upon him one Chanukah. It was the season of the Feast of Dedication and, as was his custom, he planned to preach to his people on the meaning of the feast. He had not intended to refer in his sermon either to his doubts about the Talmud or to his late discoveries in the prophecy of Daniel, but when he arose to speak, some of his deepest thoughts welled up within him and would not be denied articulation. The effect of his words upon the congregation became immediately evident.

Whispers grew to loud protests, and before the sermon progressed very far the service broke up in an uproar. That day initiated a series of petty persecutions which robbed the life of the young rabbi of its joy and made his ministry difficult to the point of impossibility.[8]

I went to a distant town and consulted a noted rabbi, who looked at me in surprise and seemed to grasp the situation. I think he knew something about the Lord Yeshua and His claims and did not want to discuss the matter, saying that if he thought and talked about the subject of the Messiah he would be discharged from his position. "But," said he, "my advice is that you go to America. There you will meet plenty of people who will tell you more about the Messiah." So intent was I upon relieving my mind of this

---

[7] *Note.* From "When Jews Face Christ," edited by Dr. Henry Einspruch, 1939, 2nd ed., p. 147-148. Copyright 1939 by American Board of Missions to the Jews, Brooklyn.
[8] *Note.* From "When Jews Face Christ," edited by Dr. Henry Einspruch, 1939, 2nd ed., p. 148-149. Copyright 1939 by American Board of Missions to the Jews, Brooklyn.

burden that I at once set sail for America, determined to find the Messiah at any cost. I did not even return to my home to inform my family that I was going.

About the middle of March, 1892, I found myself in the great city of New York. My countrymen, many of whom knew me personally at home, others by name only, gave me the kindest reception, some even leaving their business to welcome me, when they heard of my arrival. [9]

Rabbi Kline of the Hungarian Synagogue, who had preceded him to America and to whom he had a letter of recommendation, received him with much kindness. He even offered him a place of temporary service in his synagogue while awaiting a call to a suitable congregation.

On a Saturday, soon after his arrival, Rabbi Cohn went out for the customary Sabbath afternoon stroll. As had become his habit, he was meditating upon the subject of the Messiah. But in the midst of his musings, as he was passing by a church located in one of the Ghetto streets, his attention was arrested by a sign written in Hebrew and announcing "Meetings for Jews." He hardly knew what to make of the strange combination: A church with a cross upon it, and meetings for Jews!

While standing in front of the church absorbed in thought, a countryman of his seized him by the arm and said in a voice charged with fear "Rabbi Cohn, better come away from this place." The rabbi was startled, but at the same time his sense of inquiry was aroused. Just what was there about that church with

---

[9] *Note.* From "To an Ancient People: The Autobiography of Rabbi Leopold Cohn," by Rabbi Leopold Cohn, 1996, p. 9-10. Copyright 1996 by Chosen People Ministries. Reprinted with permission.

the Hebrew sign upon it? "There are apostate Jews in that church," he was told with bated breath, "and they teach that the Messiah has already come." At the sound of these words, Rabbi Cohn's pulse quickened. They teach that the Messiah has already come! Could these be the people referred to by that rabbi whom he had visited before leaving Hungary? This was something worth finding out.

As soon as he could take leave of his companion, and after making sure that he was not being observed, he quickly retraced his steps to the church. But he had hardly set foot inside the door when a sight met his eyes that compelled him to turn back. The speaker on the platform was bareheaded, and so was the audience. As it would have been to any Orthodox Jew, that was to Rabbi Cohn the height of sacrilege.[10]

On the way out, however, he thought that he should explain to the sexton his reason for leaving, and from him he received the suggestion that even if he could not stay for the service, he would nevertheless be welcome if he called for a private interview with the minister at his home.[11]

The following Monday, I called on the minister and found him a Hebrew-Believer in Messiah with a most interesting, winning way. He was educated in Talmudic literature and when he told me that he was a descendant of a certain well-known rabbi, he gained my confidence and love at once. Seeing my utter ignorance of the faith, but also my great earnestness, he gave me a Hebrew New

---

[10] *Note*. From "When Jews Face Christ," edited by Dr. Henry Einspruch, 1939, 2nd ed., p. 151-152. Copyright 1939 by American Board of Missions to the Jews, Brooklyn.
[11] *Note*. From "When Jews Face Christ," edited by Dr. Henry Einspruch, 1939, 2nd ed., p. 153. Copyright 1939 by American Board of Missions to the Jews, Brooklyn.

Covenant, asking me to read it. I opened it at once and read for the first time in my life: "This is a book of the generation of Yeshua, the Messiah, the Son of David, the Son of Abraham."

I forgot all about my troubles and became very happy, and running as fast as I could to my private room, the doors of which I locked behind me, sat down to study that book. I began reading at eleven o'clock in the morning, and continued until one o'clock after midnight. I could not understand the contents of the whole book, but I could at least realize that the Messiah's name was Yeshua, that He was born in Bethlehem, that He had lived In Jerusalem and talked to my people, and that He came just about the time indicated by the angel's message to Daniel. My joy was unbounded.

In the morning, I ran quickly to my rabbi friend, who by that time had already a prospect of securing a rabbinical charge for me, and told him of the book and my discoveries. I had not identified this Yeshua, the Messiah, with the name Jesus.

Vehemently and with terrible curses, he threw the book to the floor, stomped upon it, and in very unkind expressions, denounced me and said that that was the book which the Crucified One had made and it was the cause of all Jewish troubles. "And now," he said, "a Jew like you should not handle that book, or talk, or think of it."

I fled from his wrath with new struggles in my heart. "Is it possible that Yeshua, the Messiah, the Son of David, is the very same person whom the Non-Jews worship? Why, that is idolatry! How can I have anything to do with that?" For several days my heart ached with sorrow and depression. Then I renewed my studies and began to see the truth more plainly, as the sufferings of the Messiah were revealed to me.

The fifty-third chapter of Isaiah was a most wonderful revelation, but what of it? How could I love that hated One? How could I take His name upon my lips since He is the Crucified One and since His followers in every generation and in every country have hated my people, robbed my brothers of all that was good and fair, killed, tortured and degraded them? How could I, a true Jew, join myself to such a band of enemies of my own flesh and blood? But a small voice whispered in my heart, "If He is the One of whom the Scriptures write, then you must love Him. No matter what others do in His name, you must do as He teaches."[12]

Still halting between two opinions, Rabbi Cohn decided to fast and to pray until God clearly revealed to him what to do. When he began his supplications, he had in his hands a Tanakh. Being wholly absorbed in prayer, he was startled when the volume fell from his hands to the floor, and when he bent down to retrieve the sacred book, he saw that it had opened at the third chapter of the prophecy of Malachi, which begins with the words, *"Behold I send my messenger, and he shall prepare the way before me, and the Lord whom ye seek shall suddenly come to His temple,*

---

[12] *Note.* From "To an Ancient People: The Autobiography of Rabbi Leopold Cohn," by Rabbi Leopold Cohn, 1996, p. 12-14. Copyright 1996 by Chosen People Ministries. Reprinted with permission.

even the Angel of the Covenant whom ye delight in: behold He has already come, saith the Lord of Hosts."[13]

I fairly began to shiver; like an electric shock the words went through my whole system, and I felt as if the Crucified One stood beside me, pointing to that verse and particularly to the expression, "Behold, He has come already."

I was awestricken and fell upon my face exclaiming with all my heart, "My Lord, my Messiah, Yeshua, thou art the One in whom Israel is to be glorified. Thou art surely the One who has reconciled Thy people unto God. From this day, I will serve Thee." At that moment, a flood of light came into my mind and a stream of love to the Lord Yeshua into my heart, and straightway I went and took a meal, breaking my fast and feeling altogether a new creature.[14]

Cohn began to proclaim to all his friends and acquaintances that the rejected Jesus was the true Messiah of Israel, and that not until the Jews as a people accepted Him, could they find peace with God. The first reaction of his friends was one of amused indulgence. "Rabbi Cohn is mentally confused," they said, "due to his long separation from his loved ones." But when his perseverance and earnestness of appeal challenged their attention, they branded him as a traitor to his people and began to persecute him bitterly. Some even thought that it would be a

---

[13] *Note.* From "When Jews Face Christ," edited by Dr. Henry Einspruch, 1939, 2nd ed., p. 157. Copyright 1939 by American Board of Missions to the Jews, Brooklyn.
[14] *Note.* From "To an Ancient People: The Autobiography of Rabbi Leopold Cohn," by Rabbi Leopold Cohn, 1996, p. 15. Copyright 1996 by Chosen People Ministries. Reprinted with permission.

pious act to remove him from among the living. Such are the ways of zeal void of the knowledge of God!

When Cohn's countrymen settled down to the inevitable acceptance of the fact of his transformation, they proceeded to dispatch letters to his wife and friends at home, to inform them about his "apostasy." As a result, all communications between him and his wife were soon completely stopped.

When it became plainly evident that in New York his life would be daily in dire danger, arrangements were made for his secret departure to Scotland, that he might have opportunity to study and gather strength in a friendly environment.[15] There, through a dramatic series of events, Cohn was reunited with his wife, Rose, and two children. Although she was appalled to find the reports of his faith to be true, after heart-wrenching deliberation, she decided to remain married. Within the course of two years, she too became a vocal and dedicated believer in the Messiah.

The whole family returned to New York in the fall of 1893, feeling compelled to share the way of salvation in Yeshua the Messiah, otherwise known as Jesus.[16] To secure a platform for the proclamation of the Good News he opened a little mission in Brownsville. Being a man of practical sense, he devoted himself not alone to preaching, but also to the alleviation of the many needs that he found in the lives of immigrant Jews who were then crowding into New York by the thousands.[17]

---

[15] *Note.* From "When Jews Face Christ," edited by Dr. Henry Einspruch, 1939, 2nd ed., p. 158-159. Copyright 1939 by American Board of Missions to the Jews, Brooklyn.
[16] Editor's note.
[17] *Note.* From "When Jews Face Christ," edited by Dr. Henry Einspruch, 1939, 2nd ed., p. 162-163. Copyright 1939 by American Board of Missions to the Jews, Brooklyn.

Dr. Leopold Cohn passed away on December 19, 1937. His funeral service, held at the Marcy Avenue Baptist Church in Brooklyn, NY, and conducted by the ministerial association of which he had been a life-long member, drew a large attendance of friends and admirers, both Jews and Christians.[18]

Those who knew Dr. Cohn will remember him best for his humility of spirit.[19]

---

[18] *Note.* From "When Jews Face Christ," edited by Dr. Henry Einspruch, 1939, 2nd ed., p. 165. Copyright 1939 by American Board of Missions to the Jews, Brooklyn.
[19] *Note.* From "When Jews Face Christ," edited by Dr. Henry Einspruch, 1939, 2nd ed., p. 169. Copyright 1939 by American Board of Missions to the Jews, Brooklyn.

RABBI SAM STERN

Born: near Warsaw, Poland, circa 1918
Emigrated to Rhode Island, United States, 1952
Smikha: 1939

RABBI SAM STERN

Early Background. I was born at a time when the whole world lay in turmoil caused by World War I. People suffered hunger and starvation. Although my parents were poor at that time, they sent us boys to an expensive Orthodox religious school. I had three brothers and a sister. My father's only desire was to make rabbis of us four boys.

The Gentiles and I. My father was a rabbi. He went to the synagogue to pray three times a day. We observed the Jewish laws according to the Talmud, for our parents desired that their children, too, should follow in their father's footsteps and remain strict Orthodox Jews.

My family stayed in a little town in Congress-Poland near Warsaw. Five hundred Jewish and eight hundred Polish families lived there, but the Polish and the Jewish people were separated by these four "Chinese Walls:"

1. Clothing: Jews wore long black coats called *Kaftan* and a black hat called *Yiddishe Hutel.* The Polish people wore European clothing. It was considered a great sin for a Jew to wear European clothing.

2. Language: Jews spoke Yiddish while the Poles spoke Polish.

3. Religion: Jews worshipped in the synagogues which were also used as places of social gathering and Bible and Talmudic study classes. Polish people were almost 100 per cent Catholic.

4. Occupation: Jews were mainly blacksmiths, tailors, shoemakers, small businessmen, and owners of small hardware stores and grocery stores, while the Poles were mainly farmers and government employees. The Jews were not granted the privilege of working for the municipal and federal government, nor in factories or agriculture.

There were a thousand other differences between the Jews and the Poles—differences in customs, way of life, behaviour, temperament, and outlook. We were two peoples living in one territory, under the same wonderful Polish sky. We ate the same healthy Polish bread and breathed the same clean air. Yet we were as strange to each other as the east is from the west.

My First Acquaintance With Gentiles. When I was six years old, I tried to go for a walk outside the Jewish "Ghetto." Suddenly a Gentile boy threw a stone at me while shouting, "Jew, Jew!" I, as a child, did not know that a Jew is hated by non-Jews. Therefore, I was surprised and scared. I ran back home to mother and told her that a boy threw a stone at me, calling me, "Jew, Jew!"

"Why is the boy throwing stones at me? Why is he calling me 'Jew'? I never saw this boy before. Why does he hate me whom he had never seen before?"

"He is a Christian and Christians are Jew-haters. Even if he does not know you, he is your enemy."

"But why is he my enemy?" I kept on asking.

"He believes what he is being taught. His priest, his teacher, his parents tell him to hate the Jews. Therefore he hates you even without a cause. But when our Messiah comes, we shall be the head and not the tail. Then we will go back to Palestine and no one will persecute us anymore."

"But when will the Messiah come?" I kept on asking.

"We don't know the exact time, but He will come someday. Then our sufferings at the hands of the Christians will come to an end."

The hope of the coming of the Messiah accompanied me all my life. It gave me power to endure suffering and humiliation from my Gentile neighbours.

My Education. After my *Bar Mitzvah* I was sent to a higher rabbinical school with the sole purpose of becoming a rabbi. I spent the years from thirteen to twenty-two in different schools where the main subject was the Talmud, which consists of sixty books dealing with everyday life.

I, as a student of the Talmud, had to know by heart the name of every rabbi who expressed his opinion in the matters of damage, holidays, etc. Since there were so many to study, we did not have time for even the most elementary secular subjects. I was ignorant in matters of arithmetic, geography, etc., but at the age of twenty-two I was considered a *lamdan* which means a man who is learned in the Talmud.

Outbreak of World War II. On September 1, 1939, World War II broke out. I had just received my rabbinical diploma called *Smicha* that past summer. I planned to marry and to become a religious leader of Israel, and to use my acquired knowledge to lead my fellow Jews in the ways of the Talmudic, rabbinic traditions. The war destroyed all my plans. My very life was in danger, as was that of all my fellow Jews in Europe.

The Nazis And The Polish People. On September 4, 1939, the German soldiers came into our town.[20] Ten days before the Jewish New Year, Rosh Hashanah, four soldiers knocked at our door and burst in, saying, "All males aged fifteen to sixty are required to gather at the Kirchen Platz" (the place next to the church). My father and I hurriedly went there and found many already lying on the grass, surrounded by soldiers carrying guns. As more and more Jews joined us, we noticed the Polish people laughing and ridiculing us. "Moishe! Moishe!" they called out. Soon the soldiers ordered us to get into their military trucks which had just arrived. "Schnell!" they shouted, which meant that they wanted us to enter quickly. They hit us with their guns and rifles to make us move faster. When the trucks began to move, none of us knew our destination. We all thought that they were taking us out into the woods to be shot.[21]

After driving several hours until late at night, the trucks stopped in a big city called Konsk, and we jumped out fast. As we

---

[20] *Note.* From "Rabbis Meet Jesus the Messiah," edited by Sean O'Sullivan, p. 66. Copyright by Messianic Good News. Reprinted with permission.
[21] *Note.* From "The Victory of the Light - An Autobiography," by Sam Stern, 1987, p. 37-38. Copyright 1998 by Bible Baptist Bookstore. Reprinted with permission.

approached the gate, several soldiers who stood guarding it started to wield their rifles over our heads. Those they hit started to scream at the top of their lungs, and suddenly all of us began to scream and cry aloud, *"Oy! Oy! Wey is tsu unz!"* (Ouch! Ouch! Woe is to us!). As the screams grew louder and louder, the hundreds of crying voices blended into one great voice of despair and helplessness. There in the stillness and darkness of night, unusual voices poured from the hearts and souls of a helpless, disillusioned people, a people whose philosophy had been that man is basically good. This was the cry of a people who believed that all men are born equal. This was the voice of despair of a people who were disappointed in their religious leaders, leaders who had promised them both this world and the world to come if only they would keep the Sabbath, let their beards grow and put on the Tefilin (phylacteries) every day.[22]

If all the skies were parchment, all men writers, and all trees pens, even then it would not be possible to describe what the Nazis in co-operation with the Polish people did to the Jews in Poland. One third of the world's Jewish population was annihilated. The fields of Europe are still wet with the innocent blood that was shed. Yes, here and there a conscientious Polish family rescued a Jew, hiding him and feeding him, but the number of these good people was very small.

In May, 1945, World War II was over. The result: Nazi murderers were destroyed, Israel rose to become a nation and I had lost my entire family.

---

[22] *Note.* From "The Victory of the Light - An Autobiography," by Sam Stern, 1987, p. 39. Copyright 1998 by Bible Baptist Bookstore. Reprinted with permission.

In Search of an Answer: After the war, I came out of the concentration camp with the hope of seeing and being united with my relatives. I came to realize the bitter fact that I was alone in the world without a friend, not belonging to anybody, nobody belonging to me. I started to look for a human friend, but no one could satisfy my longing for a true mother-heart or father-love. Nobody could substitute the love of a sister, the faithfulness of a brother.

I was disappointed and desperate. I lifted my eyes up to heaven and asked the old Jewish question: Why? Why was one third of the nation of God put to death by the Nazis? Where was God when a little innocent Jewish child cried for help when the Nazi murderers raised their brutal hands to kill it? Why was God silent in these terrible times for His chosen people?

From a Displaced Persons (DP) Camp to the U.S.A. Since I had no one in Poland, I decided to go to America: I thought that perhaps in a new land I would forget the dreadful past and start a new life. In April 1946, I came to a Jewish DP Camp near the Austrian border of Germany. I registered there as a rabbi and started to work as such in the DP Camp. I also edited the DP Newspaper.[23]

One day I was walking on the Mohl Strasse, where many Jewish people gathered to sell merchandise on the black market. On this particular day at about eleven o'clock in the morning a large crowd had gathered around a speaker, and others joined to find out what he was talking about. I too came and heard the speaker say in Yiddish that the reason we Jewish people had suffered for

---

[23] *Note.* From "Rabbis Meet Jesus the Messiah," edited by Sean O'Sullivan, p. 68-69. Copyright by Messianic Good News. Reprinted with permission.

two thousand years was because we had rejected our Jewish Messiah. All my life I had never heard of Jewish people who believe in Yeshua as the Messiah, and I never imagined that I would see such a man. Soon some of the audience turned into an angry mob and began hitting him over the head with their fists and with sticks. They tore his garments and hit him until blood ran down his face. Soon the mob began to scream, "Meshumad!" (Traitor). They wanted to kill him, but instead they ran away, leaving him on the ground when police came.

This incident left me greatly disturbed. I wondered how people being Jewish could themselves persecute and beat another person for his belief. I never saw him again or spoke to him; yet his face, his personality, his loneliness—deserted by his brethren in the flesh, despised, rejected, beaten and humiliated by his own flesh and blood—are still vivid in my memory. His face is always before my eyes.[24]

Doubts and Unbelief. In 1952 I came to Rhode Island, U.S.A., where I worked as an assistant rabbi in a synagogue. Although I worked in the capacity of a Talmudic teacher in the synagogue, there was a great conflict in my heart. The question: "Why did God allow six million Jews to die?" bothered me. I taught things that I was not sure were true. I told my congregation and students: "If we Jews want to exist and to overcome our enemies we have to keep the Sabbath-day holy." In my heart I knew that 99 per cent of the Hitler-victims had kept the Sabbath-day holy, yet it did not protect them from being killed. I did not have any proof or assurance that what I taught was true. I also lost my

---

[24] *Note.* "The Victory of the Light - An Autobiography," by Sam Stern, 1987, p. 76-77. Copyright 1998 by Bible Baptist Bookstore. Reprinted with permission.

belief in the Talmudic legends, laws, and arguments pro and con. I was looking for the truth, but could not find it.

Confession Alone Is Not Enough. Each Holiday we Jews go to the synagogue and pray to God, confessing our sins, and asking for forgiveness.

We say, "Because of our sins we were driven from our land." Confession of sins is a very important part of our prayers. The Jewish prayer-book cites different kinds of sins which a Jew must confess in his daily prayers. The most solemn day of prayer is Yom Kippur, and on Yom Kippur Eve, every Jew over thirteen years of age must recite forty-five confessions called *Al Chet*. After the confession, the *Slach Lanu* (Forgive Us), is chanted by the congregation.

When I prayed these prayers I felt unhappy and dissatisfied because I knew that according to the Bible, confession alone does not forgive sin. I knew that in order for sin to be forgiven, a sacrifice called "קורבן"*(korban)* must be offered. Leviticus deals with the *korban* (קורבן) many times, especially Leviticus 5:17-19.

I was not sure that the Yom Kippur prayers have any significance in the sight of God, because I knew that right after the confessions and prayers we went back to the same old pattern of a life of sin. It seemed to me that as we were confessing our sins in the synagogue, we were mocking God. We spoke with our lips about repentance but did not really mean it. I knew that we are sinners and need a real, more valid approach to God.

Longing For The Truth. I felt very unhappy with my spiritual state of mind. I lost faith in mankind and in the rabbinical legends and teachings. I felt miserable knowing that I, as a rabbi, was teaching the people things that I did not believe. I knew that the Talmudic teachings, sayings, pilpulistic arguments, scholastic debates, hair-splitting comments about obsolete damages, laws, rules and regulations regarding Sabbath, holidays, clothing and washings, are of very little significance to us. I realized that we need some real solid spiritual truth by which to live, walk and exist as Jews. What is the truth? What is the true way for us and for me individually? I did not know!

First Contact With Light. One spring evening I walked somewhere in Rhode Island. I looked here and there without a goal, just breathing in some fresh spring air. While I strolled, I noticed some young people standing near a store handing out little printed papers. They caught my attention and handed me a pamphlet too. As I could not read English I decided to go into the store to find out what kind of sale they were having. When I came inside I was surprised to see that there was no merchandise. To my astonishment, I noticed every one sitting with eyes closed and head bowed.

"What is going on here?" I thought. I did not know that this is the manner in which Christians pray. It was in contrast to the way Jews pray—with eyes open and shaking on all sides. I waited a while till everybody had finished praying and opened their eyes. A boy came and talked to me, but I did not understand him. I had been in the United States only a few weeks and did not know the English language. Finally I said that I speak only German and Yiddish. Through the use of sign language I made a date to come back the next Wednesday, when a German-speaking person would come and explain to me what the organization was.

Love. The next Wednesday the German gentleman was waiting for me when I came. He shook my hand in a friendly manner and said to me in German, "This is a mission to the Jews."

"What is a mission?" I asked.

"The Lord sent us to the Jews to let them know that God loves them and wants them to be saved."

"What do you mean saved? How can you speak about love after the cataclysm that came over the European Jew?" I asked.

He smiled and said, "I know how you feel, but Christians, followers of Messiah, love the Jews, and all those who harm them are not Christians. The Alpha and Omega of Christianity is love to mankind, Israel included. The Lord told us to go to the Jews first."

"Weren't all those who carried crosses and had pictures of saints in their homes—yet organized pogroms against the Jews of Europe—weren't they Christians? Weren't the churches in Poland and Ukraine the main source of Anti-Semitism? Didn't the priests incite their people against the Jews?"

He looked at me and said, "The Lord teaches us to love our enemies, to show love to those who hate us. All those who do not obey the teachings of the Lord are not His followers." Then he gave me a Yiddish New Covenant and said, "Read it and you will find the true teaching of Messiah."

I took the New Covenant, put it into my pocket and said, "Yes, sir, I will read it. I want to see what the New Covenant is really like. I don't know anything at all about it."

In the next few nights I had much to read. Every line, each page, was a great revelation to me as I read with great interest. Opening the Book of Matthew, I was surprised to read that Yeshua is of the lineage of Abraham and David. I also noticed that on every page it says "As it is written," which means that it was written in our Jewish Bible. For example, in the first chapter I read that He will be born of a virgin because *it is written: "Behold a virgin shall be with child and shall bring forth a son and they shall call his name Immanuel..."* (Isaiah 7:14).

In the second chapter I read that He was born in Bethlehem as it is written, *"Thou Bethlehem in the land of Judah are not the least among the princes of Judah, for out of thee shall come forth a governor that shall rule my people Israel"* (Micah 5:2).

Also I saw that He shall come out of Egypt, for it is written, *"Out of Egypt have I called my son"* (Hosea 11:1). Thus reading I noticed on each page and in every chapter constant references to the Tanakh. It became clear to me that this book called New Covenant is actually the fulfillment of the Tanakh. I realized that we rabbis were too much occupied with the Talmud and paid little or no attention to our Holy Scriptures. Then and there I became a Bible-believing Jew. I thanked God for leading me to that little mission and decided to dedicate my life to Messiah.

My Acquaintance With A Jewish Believer. It was a few weeks before Passover. The missionary in Rhode Island gave me the address of a Jewish believer in Yeshua who lived in New York. As soon as I contacted him, he invited me to his home. He welcomed me with the greeting, "Shalom Aleichem." We read together from the New Covenant in Yiddish.

After a while he told me he had written a poem called "The Sufferer," and started to read it. But this was only a pretense, as it was in reality the fifty-third chapter of Isaiah. Then he asked me, "Who is the subject of this poem? Who suffered for our sins? By whose stripes are we healed?"

I answered, "It probably refers to Yeshua the Messiah." Then he said, "I just copied out and read to you the fifty-third chapter of Isaiah. He was the one who wrote about the Messiah."

Imagine my surprise and shock. I did not know the contents of Isaiah fifty three!

The next day I showed the same "poem" to a friend, a rabbi in New York. He did not know either that Isaiah had written the chapter. The only conclusion I could reach was that the main reason so many rabbis and other Jews don't know the Messiah, the Saviour of the Tanakh and New Covenant, is that they don't know the *Scriptures*. I decided to do everything in my power to bring the Jewish Bible to them.

The same evening I came to the Jewish believer and told him that I believe in the Bible and in the Lord Yeshua. Then and there we knelt and prayed for sin-forgiveness and for salvation. I accepted Yeshua as my personal Saviour. What a change came over me! I was very happy. I felt a peace, joy and happiness that I had never known before. My whole being turned into a happy life. I was a new creature.

My New Education. I went to Los Angeles and started my American education in the second grade of elementary school. After finishing eight grades, I graduated from high school. Later I went to Los Angeles City College, and finally to Biola College, where I received a B.A. degree. I was immersed in water according to Bible precepts, and ordained a minister of the Good News of the Messiah. Now, my deepest interest is to bring the Good News to my people, the Jews, that they too may accept their Messiah and inherit eternal life. Messiah said, *"I am the way, the truth and the life, no man cometh unto the Father except by me"* (John 14:6).

Reason. I appeal to all rabbis, leaders of the Jewish people, and Jewish laymen: Come back to our prophets, to our God and His Anointed One.

"Come now, and let us reason together, saith the LORD: though your sins be as scarlet, they shall be as white as snow; though they be red like crimson, they shall be as wool" (Isaiah 1:18).[25]

---

[25] *Note.* From "Rabbis Meet Jesus the Messiah," edited by Sean O'Sullivan, p. 69-74. Copyright by Messianic Good News. Reprinted with permission.

RABBI ISAAC LICHTENSTEIN

Born: Hungary, 1824
Died: Budapest, Hungary, October 16, 1909
Smikha: age 20, District Rabbi of Tapio-Szele, Hungary
Biography written by Henry Einspruch
with autobiographical notes

RABBI ISAAC LICHTENSTEIN

He was not yet twenty when he became a rabbi, and after officiating for several years in different communities in northern Hungary, Isaac Lichtenstein finally settled as District Rabbi in Tapio Szele. He remained there for nearly forty years, labouring ceaselessly and unselfishly for the good of his people.

Early in his ministry, a Jewish teacher in the communal school of his district casually showed him a German Bible. Turning the leaves, his eye fell on the name "Jesu Christi." He became furiously angry and sharply reproved the teacher for having such a thing in his possession. Taking the book, he flung it across the room in a rage. It fell behind others on a shelf where, dusty and forgotten, it lay some thirty-odd years.

About that time a fierce wave of Anti-Semitism broke out in Hungary, culminating in the now historic "Tisza Eslar affair." In that picturesque little Hungarian town, situated on the Theiss, twelve Jews and a Jewess were thrown into prison, accused of having killed a Christian girl in order to use her blood for ritual purposes—the most tragic part of the case being that a little Jewish boy, who had been kept some time from his parents by the police commissary, was prevailed on by threats and cruelties to appear as the chief witness against his own father (the synagogue sexton) and recite a concocted circumstantial tale of the supposed murdered girl.

As in every other case in which this diabolical charge was ever brought against the Jews, the blood accusation in Tisza Eslar was ultimately demonstrated to be false and baseless. It remains to the glory of true religion that a number of prominent Christian men, notably Dr. Franz Delitzsch, of the Leipzig University, rose to the occasion not only to defend the Jews, but also to tear the mask from all who, by their acts, scandalized Jesus in the eyes of Jewry.

The mental state of Rabbi Lichtenstein at this time is best revealed in his *Judenspiegel* (Jewish Mirror).[26]

"Often have they oppressed me from my youth, may Israel say" (Psalm 129:1). No long explanation is needed to show that in these few words the Psalmist sums up the bitter experiences and sorrows which we, at least of the older generation, have suffered from our youth up at the hands of the Christian populations surrounding us.

Mockery, scorn, blows, and all manner of humiliation, have been our portion even at the hands of Christian children. I remember still the stones which were thrown at us as we left the synagogue, and how, when bathing in the river, and powerless, we saw them cast our clothing, with laughter and insult, into the water.

---

[26] *Note.* From "When Jews Face Christ," edited by Dr. Henry Einspruch, 1932, p. 55-56. Copyright 1932 by Dr. Henry Einspruch.

Once with sorrow and weeping, I saw my father felled to the ground without the least hesitation by a nobleman, so-called, because he had not quickly enough made room for him on a narrow path. But these sad experiences are known well enough to need no dwelling on; and would to God that such persecution of the Jews by the Christians was altogether a thing of the forgotten past!

As impressions of early life take a deep hold, and as in my riper years I still had no cause to modify these impressions, it is no wonder that I came to think that Jesus Himself was the plague and curse of the Jews—the origin and promoter of our sorrows and persecutions.

In this conviction I grew to years of manhood, and still cherishing it I became old. I knew no difference between true and merely nominal Christianity; of the fountainhead of Christianity itself I knew nothing. Strangely enough, it was the horrible Tisza Eslar blood accusation which first drew me to read the New Covenant. This trial brought from their lurking places all our enemies, and once again, as in olden times, the cry re-echoed, "Death to the Jew!" The frenzy was excessive, and among the ringleaders were many who used the name of Jesus and His doctrine as a cloak to cover their abominable doings.

These wicked practices of men wearing the name of Jesus only to further their evil designs aroused the indignation of some true Christians, who, with pen on fire and warning voices, denounced the lying rage of the Anti-Semites. In articles written by the latter in defence of the Jews, I often met with passages where Messiah was spoken of as He Who brings joy to man, the Prince of peace, and the Redeemer; and His Good News was extolled as a message of love and life to all people. I was surprised and scarcely trusted my eyes when I espied in a hidden corner the New Covenant which some thirty years before I had in vexation taken from a Jewish teacher, and I began to turn over its pages and read. How can I express the impression which I then received?

Not the half had been told me of the greatness, power and glory of this Book, formerly a sealed book to me. All seemed so new, and yet it did me good, like the sight of an old friend who has laid aside his dusty, travel-worn garments, and appears in festive attire, like a bridegroom in wedding robes, or a bride adorned with her jewels."[27]

For two or three years Rabbi Lichtenstein kept these convictions locked in his own heart. He began, however, in his synagogue, to preach strange and new doctrines which both interested and astonished his hearers. At last, he could contain himself no longer. Preaching one Saturday from Messiah's parable of the whited sepulchre, he openly avowed that his subject was taken from the New Covenant and spoke of Yeshua as the true Messiah, the Redeemer of Israel. Ultimately, he embodied his ideas in three publications appearing in rapid succession, which created a tremendous sensation among the Jews, not only in Hungary, but throughout the continent of Europe. And no wonder; for here was an old and respected rabbi, still in office, calling upon his people in burning words to range themselves

---

[27] *Note.* From "A Jewish Mirror," by Rabbi Isaac Lichtenstein, 1897, *The Scattered Nation*, p.1-5. Copyright by Hebrew Christian Testimony to Israel.

under the banner of the long-despised Yeshua of Nazareth, and to hail Him as their true Messiah and King.

As was inevitable, no sooner did official Jewry realize the significance of Rabbi Lichtenstein's position and writings then a storm of persecution broke loose upon him. From the Jewish pulpit and in the press, anathemas were hurled at his head, and he who but a few weeks before was classed among the noblest leaders and teachers, was now described as a disgrace and reproach to his nation, all because he dared pronounce the hated name of Yeshua.

A slanderous report was spread that he had sold himself to the missionaries. Some even asserted that he had never written the pamphlets himself, but had only been bribed to affix his name to them. He was cited to appear before the assembled rabbinate in Budapest. On entering the hall, he was greeted with the cry, "Retract! Retract!" "Gentlemen," said the Rabbi, "I shall most willingly retract if you convince me I am wrong."

Chief Rabbi Kohn proposed a compromise. Rabbi Lichtenstein might believe whatever he liked in his heart, if he would only refrain from preaching Yeshua. As to those dreadful pamphlets which he had already written, the mischief could be undone by a very simple process. The Synod of Rabbis would draw up a document to the effect that the rabbi wrote what he did in a fit of temporary insanity. All that would be required of him would be to add his name to this statement. Rabbi Lichtenstein answered calmly but indignantly that this was a strange proposal seeing as he had only just come into his right mind. Then they demanded that he should resign from his position and be formally baptized into Christianity. He replied that he had no intention of joining any church. He had found in the New Covenant the *true Judaism,* and would remain as before with his congregation, and preach it in the synagogue.

He did so in spite of many persecutions and reproaches which were heaped upon him. From his official place as District Rabbi, he continued to teach and to preach from the New Covenant. This was a touching testimony to the strong attachment of his own community, which alone had the power to make request for his dismissal. As a matter of fact, much pressure was brought to bear upon them, and some members of the congregation and the relatives of his wife were completely ruined by loss of trade, but still they clung to him.

By this time Rabbi Lichtenstein and his writings had become widely known, and different church and missionary organizations sought his services. The Papacy too soon learned of the existence and significance of the man, and a special emissary from the Pope visited Tapio Szele with tempting offers if he would but enter the service of Rome. To all he had but one reply:

I will remain among my own nation, I love Messiah, I believe in the New Covenant; but I am not drawn to join Christendom. Just as the prophet Jeremiah, after the destruction of Jerusalem, in spite of the generous offers of Nebuchadnezzar and the captain of his host, chose rather to remain and lament among the ruins of the holy city, and with the despised remnant of his brethren, so will I remain among my own brethren, as a watchman from within and to plead with them to behold in Yeshua the true glory of Israel.

At last, however, after losing his all in the endeavour to save some of the members of his congregation from ruin, and with his health much impaired by the many trials and sorrows (as a result of his bold stand for the truth), he voluntarily resigned his office as District Rabbi.

He settled in Budapest, where he found ample scope for his talents. However, the opposition to him was relentless: He was shadowed and even physically attacked on the street. His barber was bribed with fifty Kronen to disfigure his beautiful beard. His landlord kept a close watch on everyone who visited him and reported to the rabbinical authorities.

On the other hand, he was continually interviewed and drawn into discussion by Jews from every walk of life. "Wisdom cries without and causes her voice to be heard in the street," he wrote to his friend, David Baron.

> Doctors, professors and officials, as also educated ladies, come to my house. Many families of position also visit us who condemn the harsh conduct of the rabbinate here in relation to me. Many foreigners also visit me. I have often very grave, important discussions with Talmudists and rabbis from a long distance, who wish to bring me to a compromise; and it is worthy to note that many who had formerly no knowledge of the New Covenant and stared blankly and incredulously at me when I quoted its sublime doctrines, have afterwards begged to possess one.

For over twenty years Rabbi Lichtenstein witnessed in many parts of the continent to the truth as he saw it in Yeshua the Messiah. At last, the storms of controversy, of misunderstanding and antagonism, began to tell on him. His spirit, however, remained undaunted. About this time he wrote:[28]

Dear Jewish brethren, I have been young, and now am old. I have attained the age of eighty years, which the Psalmist speaks of as the utmost period of human life on earth. When others of my age are reaping with joy the fruit of their labours, I am alone, almost forsaken, because I have lifted up my voice in warning, "O Israel, turn to the Lord thy God, for thou hast fallen by thine iniquity. Take these words and turn thee to the Lord thy God. Kiss the Son, lest He be angry, and ye perish from the way."

I, an honoured Rabbi for the space of forty years, am now, in my old age, treated by my friends as one possessed by an evil spirit, and by my enemies as an outcast. I have become a butt of mockers who point the finger at me. But while I live I will stand on my watchtower, though I may stand there all alone. I will listen to the words of God, and look for the time when He will return to Zion in mercy, and Israel shall fill the world with his joyous cry, "Hosanna to the Son of David. Blessed is He that cometh in the name of the Lord! Hosanna in the highest!"[29]

Quite unexpectedly he was taken ill and lingered only a short while. As he realized that his end was approaching, in the presence of his wife and the nurse, he said:

---

[28] *Note.* From "When Jews Face Christ," edited by Dr. Henry Einspruch, 1932, p. 59-64. Copyright 1932 by Dr. Henry Einspruch.
[29] *Note.* From "A Jewish Mirror," by Rabbi Isaac Lichtenstein, 1897, *The Scattered Nation*, p.21-22. Copyright by Hebrew Christian Testimony to Israel.

Give my warmest thanks and greetings to my brethren and friends; goodnight, my children; goodnight, my enemies, you can injure me no more. We have one God and one Father of all who are called children in heaven and on earth, and one Christ (Anointed One, Messiah) who gave up His life on the cursed tree for the salvation of men. Into Thy hands I commend my spirit.

The day was dismal; it was eight o'clock in the morning on Friday, October 16, 1909, that the venerable rabbi entered into the presence of his Lord.[30]

Excerpts from Personal Letters - From R. Lichtenstein to his son Dr. Emmanuel Lichtenstein

By His divine providence I accidentally took in my hand a New Covenant which for many long years I had left unnoticed in a corner. From every line, from every word, the Jewish spirit streamed forth: light, life, power, endurance, faith, hope, love, chastity; limitless, indestructible faith in God; kindness to prodigality; moderation to self-denial; content to the exclusion of all sense of need; pity, gentleness, consideration for others, with extreme strictness as regards self; all these were to be found pervading the book.

Every noble principle, every pure moral teaching, all patriarchal virtues with which Israel was adorned in its prime, and is still to some extent adorned as heir of the community of Jacob, I found in this book of books refined

---

[30] *Note.* From "When Jews Face Christ," edited by Dr. Henry Einspruch, 1932, p. 65. Copyright 1932 by Dr. Henry Einspruch.

and simplified, and that in it there is balsam for every pain of soul, comfort for every sorrow, healing for every moral hurt—renewal of faith, and resurrection to a new life well-pleasing to God.[31]

I had thought the New Covenant to be impure, a source of pride, of overweening selfishness, of hatred, of the worst kind of violence: but as I opened it, I felt myself peculiarly and wonderfully taken possession of. A sudden glory, a light, flashed through my soul. I looked for thorns, and I gathered roses; I discovered pearls instead of pebbles; instead of hatred, love; instead of vengeance, forgiveness; instead of bondage, freedom; instead of pride, humility; instead of enmity, conciliation; instead of death, life, salvation, resurrection, heavenly treasure.[32]

The Jew has been sick for two thousand years; in vain has he sought healing and help of his physicians; in vain has he spent all his substance. By faith alone, and by contact with Yeshua, by the power which goes forth from Yeshua, can he find healing. I would point him to Yeshua in His heavenly glory, in His divinity, exalted and great as eternity, as the Redeemer, the Messiah, the Prince of Peace.[33]

I said, *"Days should speak, and multitude of years should teach wisdom. But there is a spirit in man, and the breath of the Almighty giveth them understanding"* (Job 32:7-8).

---

[31] *Note.* From "Two Letters; or What I Really Wish," by Rabbi Isaac Lichtenstein, p. 15. Copyright by Hebrew Christian Testimony to Israel.

[32] *Note.* From "Two Letters; or What I Really Wish," by Rabbi Isaac Lichtenstein, p. 3-4. Copyright by Hebrew Christian Testimony to Israel.

[33] *Note.* From "Two Letters; or What I Really Wish" by Rabbi Isaac Lichtenstein, p. 27. Copyright by Hebrew Christian Testimony to Israel.

When the Council and the high priests in Jerusalem considered means to silence Peter and the Apostles, a Pharisee of the name of Gamaliel, greatly esteemed by all the people, stood up in the Council, and said: *"Let [these men] alone, for if this plan or this work is of men, it will come to nothing; but if it is of God, you cannot overthrow it"* (Acts 5:27-39, quoted from 38-39). The work was of God, for it has not perished in the course of time; the holy fire has neither been suppressed nor extinguished by the many storms which have raged against it, but it has kindled the more, and during eighteen centuries has shone even brighter and more clearly, filled with the most ennobling thoughts, and ever extending its dominion with the forward movements of the times.

The Good News of Messiah has outrun Alexander, who stopped at the Indus; it has outrun Crassus, who stopped at the Euphrates; it has outrun Varus, who stopped at the Rhine; it has outrun every world conqueror, and will only come to a stop when it has reached Israel.

The sun also rises, and the sun goes down, And hastens to the place where it arose. The wind goes toward the south, And turns around to the north; The wind whirls about continually, And comes again on its circuit (Eccl. 1:5-6).[34]

---

[34] *Note.* From "Two Letters; or What I Really Wish," by Rabbi Isaac Lichtenstein, p.18. Copyright by Hebrew Christian Testimony to Israel.

Extract from a Published Personal Interview

I never knew God until I knew the Messiah. God to me was only a stern judge. Now in Messiah I know Him as an unspeakably mercifully and infinitely loving Father. Through Messiah I throw off all care as a bird after a dip in the river shakes off the drops of water from its wings. My enemies have in mockery called me "a missionary" and I have replied: "Yes, I am a missionary in the sense in which Abraham was a missionary; in the sense in which everyone is a missionary who seeks to lead men into and along the right way. If I strive to lead men into the Truth as it is in Yeshua, I am a missionary." And so a rabbi wrote to me lately: "You have shown us the ladder that leads up to heaven." That is my mission. Surely we have ten thousand promises in the firmament of Scripture, bright as the stars on the brow of night, to kindle and sustain our hope that the Jews will soon come in great numbers to the Lord Yeshua the Messiah, the great and good Physician, and that they will touch the hem of his garment, and receive from Him all the healing, all the strength, and all the joy that they need for their magnificent mission on earth and ministry in heaven.[35]

---

[35] *Note.* From "Memories of Gospel Triumphs Among the Jews in the Victorian Era," by John Dunlop, 1894, p. 485-486. Copyright 1894 by S.W. Partridge & Co.

Ornate stained glass from Temple Synagogue
Miodowa 24 Kraków Poland

RABBI DANIEL WEISS

Born: Poland
Autobiography

RABBI P. DANIEL WEISS

I was born in Poland where my father was a respected rabbi, and my mother was a pious woman who spoke Hebrew as well as Polish fluently.

After some years at a Talmudic school, where I had studied many other subjects after class, I returned home. I did not, however, intend staying at home because my opinions and way of thinking had changed. I had no inner peace anymore. I used to be very interested in the Talmud and other Jewish classical writings, meditating on them, but then had become engrossed in the prophecies of the Tanakh. Again I had studied the *aggadot* (Jewish traditions) and began to doubt; perhaps the writers of the Talmud had made a big mistake by condemning the greatest man of their nation to death; maybe they had had some reason for inventing the most fantastic tales about His birth.

The more I studied the *aggadot,* the clearer my insight became till at last the exalted, though terrifying, thought occurred to me that He is indeed the promised Messiah. I compared the explanations of the Talmud with the prophecies of the Tanakh and saw that all foretold by the holy prophets had from beginning to end been fulfilled in the life of Yeshua.

From that time I did not have any peace of mind but somehow lacked the courage to reveal the secret of my heart to anybody, knowing that my voice would be like that of a preacher in the desert.

I was still young and thus kept everything secret for a while. However, one day I heard Jewish people telling nasty stories about the Saviour and I became so agitated that I could hardly control myself. I went home and my mother could tell by my face that something unpleasant must have happened. I did not want to tell her but when she insisted, I revealed to her what had been going on in my mind. In anger and consternation she cried out: "Do you really know what you are saying? The devil has taken possession of you to draw you away from the Lord. What shall be your fate on the day of judgment?" But when she noticed that she would get nowhere with hard words, she pleaded with me to get rid quickly of those ideas while there was still time. My reply was that up to that day I had never grieved her, but had always taken trouble to please her, and the way I was now causing her to worry, must be proof of my conviction of the truth. Therefore, I could not change my way of thinking. Before I had finished speaking, my father entered the room and we kept quiet. During the night my parents awoke and started to talk about me. After that I was carefully watched by them and when they saw me reading a book other than the Talmud, it was burned. This went on for a year.

One day my father spoke very severely to me. I told him that no threats or curses would ever change my mind. This was the first of many long discussions which made life very unpleasant. Considered to be such a great sinner, I was regarded as being the cause of every affliction and grief. Eventually, I ran away from home to my uncle in Lodz.

He was a rich man, had no children and was pleased to have me stay with him; but after the receipt of a letter from my father telling him about me, he changed so much that I had to leave him. Then friends invited me to stay with them. I earned my keep by teaching while I continued studying. At last, I passed my examination and became a rabbi.

A friend invited me to a Baptist church where a missionary was to speak. We went and heard him address a large gathering in words full of spirit and truth. Afterwards, when I confirmed the truth of the missionary's words there was an uproar. The other Jewish hearers cursed me and wanted to tear me to pieces so that I had to hide myself. The next day I left Lodz and travelled to Vilna where I continued my studies. My parents had, however, given me a wife when I was still very young, and so I was obliged to accept the office of a rabbi in a small Polish town. It was the beginning of a difficult time for me.

On the Sabbath before the Passover I had to speak in a synagogue in Chomez. In my pocket was a New Covenant and a Hebrew book of the same size. By mistake I took out the New Covenant and dropped it. It was picked up by somebody near me, and when he wanted to hand it to me, he saw that it was a New Covenant. He screamed as if a snake had bitten him, and told the congregation that I, their rabbi, possessed a New Covenant. He added that not only I but they also would be punished for my sin. This made me tell them that I was going to resign from my office as their rabbi, which I did a few days later.

What I had to suffer at that time! My mother died of worry and my father decided not to see me again. Afterwards, I was appointed as a religious instructor and teacher of Hebrew by the Jewish congregation in Warsaw, a vocation I practiced for nine years. Then HK, a former teacher, was appointed inspector of religious instructors. One day, he and my colleagues were gathered in my classroom for a discussion when the sorry plight of the Russian Jews cropped up. We considered ways to improve their position.

I openly said that the position of us Jews would only improve greatly if we received our Messiah, Yeshua who had shed His blood on Golgotha to liberate us from our sins. This started a discussion, but not an angry one, because all my colleagues present were free-thinkers and the inspector himself an avowed atheist. He had hated me for a long time and now seized the opportunity to report me to the Board of the Jewish congregation.

When I attended a Sunday evening service of the Warsaw Mission, two young Jewish men entered the hall. Afterwards, they went to the Jewish congregation to tell them that I was an immersed Jew and they had seen me kneel with others in church. The Board met and decided to dismiss me without any remuneration or compensation, and without the opportunity of defending myself. It took a long time before any compensation was promised to me.

When I appeared before the Board to receive the money, I asked them: "Why was I dismissed before any investigation had been made?" One of the Board members answered: "If we had asked you to come, you would not have told the truth. Now we do not believe you any longer in the matter, because two witnesses have, according to Jewish law, sworn before a rabbi to the truth of their statement, and you have forfeited your right to be believed." To this I replied: "Gentlemen, you are mistaken; I am always ready to speak the truth." "Did you pray with the Christians and kneel with them? Were you ceremonially immersed in water some time ago?" I answered calmly: "I have not yet been immersed but hope that it will happen soon." That was enough; I was not allowed to say another word; and was bombarded with abusive language and ridicule. But I remained calm and respectful.

During the ensuing pause, one of the men jumped up, turned to me and screamed: "You trouble-maker, how dare you utter those religious opinions so calmly and defiantly in our presence? We know that as former rabbi you will attack us verbally and in writing and slander Jewry, you wicked traitor." One of the men ran to me, his hand raised ready to hit me, and shouting: "Yes, it would be best to kill him." My reply was: "Gentlemen, I am in your power and you are free to do it. I do not hate you; no, on the contrary, I love you. But I sincerely regret that you are so stubborn, and do not want to admit that much evil has happened to us because we had slandered and crucified our Redeemer."

Now the excitement flared up once more and I was not allowed to say another word. One of them, however, asked me: "If the congregation should take you back and pay you a good salary on condition that you promise not to contact the missionaries again, would you be willing to do it?" To this proposal I answered: "I shall never sell my soul for money."[36]

---

[36] *Note.* From "Rabbis Meet Jesus the Messiah," edited by Sean O'Sullivan, p. 81. Copyrighted by Messianic Good News. Reprinted with permission.

RABBI HAROLD VALLINS

Born: United Kingdom, April 6, 1941
Died: Melbourne, Australia, June 2, 2009
Smikha: 1970

Rabbi Harold Vallins

I was born on the 6th of April, 1941, and for the first four years of my life, I, and my brother Michael, (less than a year younger than me) lived in Wales. Sadly my father died when I was only four years old and the family then moved back to London in 1944.

My mother married again and the family moved to Ilford in Essex just outside of London. It was here that we stayed for the rest of our childhood. My family belonged to an Orthodox synagogue although we were not Orthodox in practice. We attended the Synagogue on the main festival days and little else. My brother and I attended *cheder* (religious classes) where we were taught to read Hebrew and also learned about Jewish customs and rituals.

After the war, news filtered through that the Jewish population of Europe had been decimated. We began to see the horrific photographs of the concentration camps. We blamed Christianity for the Holocaust. So it was no wonder that we grew up not wanting anything to do with Yeshua or Christianity.

I had my Bar Mitzvah at the age of thirteen, but because of the terribly cruel way my rabbi treated me, I left the synagogue and vowed never to return. For the next seven years, I remained a confirmed "fanatical atheist." Then I met and fell in love with a girl who asked me to accompany her to a dance that was being held at her Synagogue youth club. I told her that I had vowed never to enter a Synagogue again. She gave me a choice: "Come with me to my club or we don't go out together!" Well, being a man of high principle—I went to the Synagogue with her!

It was a Reform Synagogue and it was there that I met a young and dynamic rabbi who showed me that Judaism could be open, wonderful, loving and kind. Rabbi Dow (pronounced Dov) showed me a God who was kind and merciful and he got me talking with God again. I was so impressed with this rabbi and synagogue that I eventually took over the running of his youth group. Four years later I enrolled at the Leo Baeck Theological College of Judaic Studies in London. After eight long years of full time study, I was finally ordained as a rabbi in 1970.[37]

My first synagogue was a bad experience. I found the congregation to be very reactionary and very hostile to people who wanted to convert to Judaism. It came to a head when one member of the congregation asked me to conduct a funeral service for his son who wanted to marry a non-Jewish girl. I refused and a furious disagreement broke out that eventuated in my leaving.

I was truly broken, angry with God, disillusioned and very depressed. In October 1972 I returned to London and was

---

[37] See "Melbourne Rabbi Who Became Christian Dies," by Peter Kohn, 2009, *The Australian Jewish News*, for more information.

admitted into hospital with a nervous breakdown. Later, after being threatened with electric shock treatment, I discharged myself from that hospital. I then met a wonderful therapist Irene Bloomfield, and the next two years of my life were among the best I can remember. With her kindness and her wonderful knowledge, I discovered many of my weaknesses and my strengths and I eventually trained with Irene to become a counsellor myself.

In 1974, I took a position as rabbi in a synagogue in the East End of London. At the same time, I married my first wife, and we settled down and had two children. In 1981, we responded to an invitation to move to Australia and lead a congregation in the southern suburbs of Melbourne. Sadly, the move to Australia did not have a good effect upon my marriage and my wife and I were divorced in 1983. However, we remained good friends and we agreed to share equal custody of our children.

It was during this time that I met Rev. Gerald Rose, a minister at a nearby Church of Christ. We met regularly and established a very close friendship. Gerald came to speak at my synagogue and he invited me to speak in his church. It was a very nourishing exchange of ideas and philosophies. Truly, I began to feel as if I had far more in common with Gerald than I did with my own rabbinical colleagues.

These differences with my own colleagues eventuated in my being voted out of my congregation. However, the families that supported me asked me to start a new synagogue and in 1991 Bet Hatikvah (House of Hope) Synagogue was formed.

It was here that I remarried in 1992. It was during this time that I began to explore alternative religions and philosophies. I met with a Japanese group called Sukyo Mahikari and an Indian group who followed the teaching of Sai Baba. These groups taught me about humility and the universality of religion.

It was in November 1997 that I noticed my friend and member of the congregation, Brian, undergoing a complete change of character. He had been a very hard-headed businessman and I began to see a much softer, more compassionate person emerging. When I asked him what was causing the change, he was somewhat reluctant to discuss it. I pestered him about it and eventually he told me that he had attended a Prayer Breakfast in Washington D.C. and that, as a result, he was now meeting with a group of men once a week for breakfast, Bible-study and prayer.

This interested me a great deal and I asked if I could come. Brian said, "No!" I pestered him for a few weeks until he finally relented and let me attend a meeting. I found the group was made up of followers of Yeshua, which was why Brian had been a little reluctant to invite me. But instead of being turned off, I really enjoyed the experience and became a regular attendee.

I now found myself being forced to confront all my earlier concepts about Yeshua. I had already begun to question my inner-feelings about Yeshua through my friendship with Gerald Rose, but these remained inner-questions and I had never publicly expressed these thoughts.

What really impressed me about this group were the sincere and impromptu prayers that they offered and which were not read from any prayer books. This was strange to me for Jews have always read their prayers from a prayer book. Impromptu prayer in Judaism, was a rare event. But these men recited their prayers from their hearts, as if they were "chatting" with God or Yeshua rather than reciting.

After a few weeks, I was asked to conclude the breakfast with a prayer. I freaked out! I had no prayer book with me and I had not the faintest idea of what to say. I desperately tried to remember some of the prayers I had heard and used as many of their words as I could. As I came to the end, I found myself concluding the prayer with the words, "Through Jesus Christ our Lord, Amen."

It took me a week to recover from that! I didn't dare tell anyone what I had done. I had been brought up never to mention the name of Yeshua and now I had prayed to "Him!"

I decided the best thing to do was to stay quiet about the whole thing and not to say a word to anyone.

Some weeks later, I was invited by the members of my prayer group to go with them to the U.S. Presidential Prayer Breakfast in Washington, D.C. It was to be one of the most significant journeys I had ever undertaken.

On the third day of our visit we met up with all the other delegates from our region and we had a wonderful meal after which we all sat around in a circle and each person gave some of their background to the group. At the end of the evening, we all stood up and held hands as we were led in prayer. As the prayer was being recited, I felt as though I was being transformed onto another plane of life. I suddenly knew that Yeshua was in the room with us.

I could actually feel Yeshua come and stand behind me and put His hand upon my shoulder. And I could hear myself saying, inside my head, "Yeshua, you are my Messiah, my Lord, my Saviour!" I felt tears in my eyes and felt my whole body was trembling. It was such a unique and awe-inspiring moment. But I still did not tell anyone. I was unsure? Unconvinced? I guess I was very afraid.

The next day, as I was coming into the hotel, a lady came up to me and gave me a piece of paper. She said that the Lord had urged her to give it to me. I opened up the folded sheet and on it was written:

> Now the word of the LORD came to me saying, "Before I formed you in the womb I knew you, and before you were born I consecrated you; I appointed you a prophet to the nations."
>
> Then the LORD put out his hand and touched my mouth; and the LORD said to me, "Now I have put my words in your mouth.
>
> "See, today I appoint you over nations and over kingdoms, to pluck up and to pull down, to destroy and to overthrow, to build and to plant" (Jeremiah 1: 4-5 & 9-10).

She could not have known that I had written my main rabbinical thesis on "The Life and the Personal Inner Struggles of the Prophet Jeremiah."

I felt that this was a message from God. He was calling me to pluck up and pull down, destroy and overthrow all that I had learnt so far about my religious life. Only after that would I be able to build and to plant. I experienced a little of what Moses had felt that day he stood before the burning bush; how Jeremiah felt when he was being called. I was very anxious and worried.

The next day, I decided to visit the Holocaust Museum. I felt that it was a chance for me to get back in touch with reality; with my Jewish roots. After all, the Holocaust was one of the prime causes of much of the animosity felt by the Jews towards the Christians. Perhaps I would feel the same?

Whilst I was walking around the museum, another woman, a complete stranger, came and asked me if I was the rabbi from Melbourne. When I told her who I was, she also gave me a piece of paper saying that the Lord had urged her to give me this message. I opened up the folded piece of paper and it read:.

"The days are surely coming," says the LORD, "when I will make a new covenant with the house of Israel and the house of Judah. It will not be like the covenant that I made with their ancestors when I took them by the hand to bring them out of the land of Egypt—a covenant that they broke, though I was their husband," says the LORD.

"But this is the covenant that I will make with the house of Israel after those days," says the LORD, "I will put my law within them, and I will write it on their hearts; and I will be their God, and they shall be my people" (Jeremiah 31:31-33).

It was obvious to me now that God was directing me along a completely new path. I went back to the hotel and prayed and thanked God. God was putting a new heart in me and was showing me a new path, a path that I was to walk with God's Son, Yeshua. Strangely, I felt somewhat numb, as if this experience was not supposed to happen to someone like me. I wasn't at all sure how to react and I was still very anxious. I had accepted Yeshua as my Messiah and my Saviour, but what was supposed to happen next?

The next day I took myself off to the Holocaust museum again. I had this strong urge to know and understand why I had grown up blaming Yeshua and Christianity for the Crusades, the Inquisition and the Holocaust, and yet here I was, willing to accept Yeshua as my Messiah. The whole history of persecution that the Jews had suffered came pouring into my brain. Where was Justice? Where was Goodness? Where was Love? Where, oh where was God?

On the last night of the Presidential Prayer Breakfast they held a special "Family Dinner." I found my mind wandering and I began to see those terrible scenes I had witnessed at the Holocaust Museum. But then, I felt something stir inside me. Amidst all the euphoria of the Family Dinner, I had received just small glimpse of why it all happened and I had a great urge to tell everyone what I had come to realize.

I suddenly found myself walking on to the stage right up to where the speaker was speaking. He finally gave me a chance to address the audience and I told them that I was a rabbi and that I had just become aware of whom Yeshua was and accepted him into my life as my Saviour and Messiah. I also explained to them my struggle with the Holocaust and that I had just come to realize that what had happened was that too many people, across the face of Europe, had removed God from their lives. When a whole community or country removes God and Yeshua from their lives, they become capable of inflicting the most indescribable evil upon each other. Life without God has no meaning, no value and therefore, human beings also come to have no value if the propaganda is skilfully used.

I also remember announcing that although I had become a disciple of Yeshua, I would need their prayers as I had to return home and tell my wife and family, synagogue and community. I was very emotional and all I can remember is that everyone was standing and that this incredible love was being poured over me. It was truly overwhelming and has been ever since.

The next day I had to begin my journey home, such a changed person from the Harold who had come to Washington. On the way home to Australia, I stopped off first in London to see my mother. However, try as I might, I just could not bring myself to tell her. She was not in the best of health and I was afraid that at her age, she would find it too much of a terrible shock. So I left London without telling her.

I then went to Toronto to visit my brother, Michael. I spent a whole day praying that Yeshua would give me the right words to say. Just after dinner I finally announced, "Michael, I have to tell you that I have accepted Yeshua into my life as my Messiah and my Saviour and that I am now a follower of Yeshua." Mike, his wife, Chris and their three children all jumped up and exclaimed, "Halleluyah! We have been praying for this for years!"

I was dumbfounded and asked: "What do you mean?" He replied, "I've been a believer for over twelve years!" "How come you didn't tell me before?" I asked. Mike quickly answered: "I should tell my brother, a rabbi, that I believe in Yeshua? Well, we all laughed and celebrated and gave praise and thanks to the Lord. It was an amazing week I spent with them.

However, when I returned to Australia and told my wife, she was devastated. She is very committed to Judaism and her pain was compounded by the fact that she was the cantor at the Bet Hatikvah Synagogue. When my congregation found out, they felt they had no alternative but to ask me to resign. They were very bewildered and hurt. They felt betrayed and thoroughly let down. I lost many friends within the congregation and more as the news began to spread.

It was amazing though, that one of the members of Bet Hatikvah, Ike, offered me a job because he knew I would have no income. Without Ike's generosity and altruism, I would have been in serious difficulty. I praise the Lord that he moved Ike in such a way.

It was soon after this that I first heard the term "Messianic Jews" and I found myself attending a conference of Messianic Jews in America. It was a great experience and I discovered that it was not only possible to remain Jewish and still have Yeshua as my Messiah, but that it was also highly desirable. After all, Yeshua was a Jewish Messiah and all His early followers were Jewish. Yeshua did not come to abolish Judaism but to fulfill it. When the blindfold is removed, it is just awesome to see Yeshua prophesied in the Old Testament; and to see Yeshua in each of the Jewish festivals giving them new meaning, new life. In other words, I have not ceased being a Jew, but now, I am a complete Jew believing in a Jewish Messiah.

I have now found a wonderful family in the ministry of Celebrate Messiah and in the congregation of Beit HaMashiach. They are very special people and they have given me so much love and support.

I see my two children regularly and I must say they are such beautiful children. I derive so much pleasure from them, and I feel blessed by them. My wife and I remain good friends and we will always be so.

Although this last year has had much pain and sadness, I am excited about my journey with the Messiah. The pain and suffering I have experienced has made me a better person, certainly, more able to understand the suffering that Yeshua experienced. I am now blessed by the fact that Yeshua died for my sins; that Yeshua saved me by dying on the cross and thus He has given me so much purpose and direction in my life. I have much hope and expectation for the future. I really feel "called" by Yeshua and I feel just a great sense of awe that He has chosen me for a task that He has set-aside for me.

Harold R. Vallins
Melbourne Australia[38]

[38] *Note.* From "Harold Vallins Dies in Melbourne," by Dr. Chris Field, 2009, http://chrisfieldblog.com/2009/06/04/rabbi-harold-vallins. Reprinted with permission.

CHIL SLOSTOWSKI

Born: Poland, early 1900's
Smikha: Dubno, Poland at age 25
Autobiography

RABBI CHIL SLOSTOWSKI

As a descendant of a number of Orthodox rabbis, I received a strict rabbinical education. I thank God for a mind which enabled me at the age of seventeen years to obtain the highest diplomas of two rabbinical seminaries. These distinctions, however, did not satisfy me and I continued earnestly to study the Talmud, the *Shulchan Aruch,* and other rabbinical works. When I was twenty years old, I knew much of the Talmud and other commentaries on the Tanakh by heart. On account of my thorough knowledge of those books, many rabbis used to consult me concerning *Kashrut* (dietary law) questions, and in spite of my youth they accepted my decisions as correct.

At the age of twenty-five I became rabbi at Dubno in Poland. I was strictly Orthodox and rejected every opinion that did not comply with the letter of Talmudic traditions. Two years later I had a call to Lodz, a large town in Poland. There I held not only the position of a rabbi, but became also a Professor at the Rabbinical Seminary. In my lectures I admonished the students to abhor Christianity and Yeshua Himself. I believed all the terrible stories about Yeshua as contained in the Talmud.

77

Through God's wise foresight, however, I became acquainted at that time with a well-educated missionary. He knew the Talmud and began to converse with me. What he told me was very interesting so that I paid him frequent visits. Very soon my relatives got to know about this and became very perturbed. They discussed the matter and then decided to write, without my knowledge, to the Chief Rabbi of Palestine, T. Cook. Rabbi Cook knew my name through our *Kashrut* correspondence. He was told of "the great danger which threatened my soul," because of my association with a Christian missionary. They implored him to have pity on my soul and to save me from "the great danger" by extending to me a call to Palestine, and obtaining for me a permit to enter the land.

They were convinced that in that way I would be "quickly delivered from the bad influence of the dangerous missionary." During all that time I had not the slightest idea of what was going on.

A few weeks later I received a letter from the Chief Rabbi. He wrote about various things and mentioned quite casually that he could get me a permit to enter Palestine should I wish to come there. I was delighted at the prospect of going to the land of my forefathers, and accepted his suggestion joyfully. A month later I went to Palestine.

Shortly after my arrival, the Chief Rabbi appointed me as Secretary to the Chief Rabbinate of Jerusalem. Moreover, he continually showed me his special favour and liked to have me near him. His interest in me became so obvious that I began to wonder what might be the reason. One day I frankly asked him about this. Then he told me of the correspondence with my relatives, and tried to convince me of the "falseness" of the missionary's teachings.

Here I must confess that the missionary's words had penetrated only my mind and not my heart. Sometimes the truth takes many years to proceed from the head into the heart, and so it was in my case.

In consequence of the Chief Rabbi's talks, I began to think that he might be right, and gradually the missionary's conversations with me faded from my mind.

After the death of Rabbi Cook I accepted a call as Talmud teacher at the Rabbinical Seminary of Tel Aviv where I taught for two years. Yet the Lord sought me!

One day I travelled in the company of several members of my committee by train from Haifa to Jerusalem. Opposite me in our compartment there sat a young man reading in a little book. On the cover I could see very clearly the words "ברית חדשה" (New Covenant in Hebrew). At once I knew that he was a Jewish believer in Yeshua; Jewish, because he read Hebrew and a believer in Yeshua, because he read the New Covenant.

In the presence of the members of my committee I felt obliged to protest to the young man and to reproach him for reading such a strictly forbidden book as the New Covenant. I criticized him severely and in that way made known my position as rabbi. To my surprise the young man did not get annoyed but smiled at me and said: "Perhaps you will show me what you find offensive in the book and I will try to explain it."

When he had said that, my thoughts suddenly went back over the years to the time when I had read a little in the New Covenant though it had been only superficially without reaching my heart. Nevertheless, I knew there was nothing repugnant in the book. What annoyed me most at that moment was the presence of my fellow travellers. I had to give the young man a suitable reply so as not to lose my friends' respect.

That was why I said to him: "How can I show you wrong statements in a book which we are forbidden to read?!" He answered: "How can you criticize and judge something of which you have no knowledge? First read the book please, and then you will see that there is nothing whatsoever in it that could be criticized." I remained silent, for what could I have said? Was I not well aware in my heart and soul that there was not a single word in the New Covenant which could be criticized or condemned?

Suddenly, my discussions with the missionary in Poland came back to my mind. Why had I run away from his instructions which I had respected so much? Like lightning these thoughts moved within my soul. Obviously, the young man noticed the confused expression in my eyes. He whispered to me: "I see you are interested in these things. May I give you this New Covenant? Please take it. I have another one at home. Your companions do not see it. Just now they are looking out of the window admiring the fields." Quickly I took the little book and put it in my pocket.

That same evening I began reading the New Covenant in my room in Jerusalem. Before opening it, however, I had prayed:

"Open thou mine eyes, that I may behold wondrous things out of thy law" (Psalm 119:18).

In His loving-kindness the Lord heard my prayer and showed me things which I had never seen before. While reading I felt the creation of a clean heart and of a right spirit within me (Psalm 51:10) and there was new light (Psalm 119:105). Like a thirsty man drinks greedily when he has found a spring of fresh, cool water, so I drank in page after page of the New Covenant. In one long draught I read the Good News of Matthew, Mark and Luke until I noticed the clock—3 a.m.!

With every page there grew and deepened the conviction that Yeshua is the Messiah prophesied to us Jews. Slowly but surely my burdened heart, soul and spirit became free and joyful. This was an entirely new and strange feeling for which I could find no name at the time. I could not have described it, yet it was so real. Certain chapters of the Holy Scriptures attracted me in a special way and I can recollect still many of them. The Sermon on the Mount opened up before me a new world, a world full of beauty and glory. The Proclaimer of such a lovely world cannot be evil, whatever the Talmud says. The words, *"Heaven and earth shall pass away, but my words shall not pass away"* could have been spoken only by God Himself or by a madman. And from the answers that Yeshua gave the Scribes and Pharisees, it is abundantly clear that He was not a lunatic but, on the contrary, exceptionally wise. Therefore, it cannot be otherwise but fact that He was truly God, as also His disciples maintained (John 20:28). I was deeply impressed also by Luke 23:34, *"Then said Yeshua, Father, forgive them; for they know not what they do."* Compare this utterance with that of Jeremiah when he was oppressed. Jeremiah was enraged and cursed his persecutors.

Yeshua, on the other hand, even when nailed to the Tree of Sacrifice, had nothing but forgiveness, mercy, sympathy and prayer for His persecutors. What a difference! How much greater was He than the prophets were!

My soul was so touched by what I had read that, although it was three o'clock in the morning, for the first time in my life I knelt down and prayed; for we Jews pray standing and not kneeling. I cannot say how long I prayed but I know that never before had I prayed with such fervour and purpose. I wept and implored God for light. I beseeched Him to show me the truth: what was right and what was wrong, the Talmud or the New Covenant. And for the first time I prayed in the Name of YESHUA!

After that prayer there came into my heart such peace and joy as I had never experienced before, not even on Yom Kippur (the Day of Atonement), although on that day I always fasted and prayed fervently. Never before had I felt such certainty of reconciliation with God as I felt then and, thank God, that feeling has remained with me ever since. I knew and had no doubt whatever that the Lord Yeshua is the long-prophesied Messiah of the Jews and the Saviour of the world, and I came to see in Him my personal Redeemer.

Then I went to bed but after this vivid experience I was unable to sleep. Soon I heard a voice say to me: "Never again wander away from Me! I will use you for the glory of My name and as a witness to My saving grace." This was no imagination but fact, and immediately I answered: "Lord, here am I."

From then onward, my life no longer belonged to me but to Him and so it is still. For in that solemn moment I surrendered myself completely and unreservedly to Him. Even that, I felt, was little enough as repayment for all He had done for me when He saved my soul from eternal damnation.

Alas, at first I was no more than a secret believer. In my inward being I knew that the Lord Yeshua was the Messiah of Israel and my personal Redeemer but continued nevertheless to fulfill my tasks and duties as rabbi. Two months I lived like this. But oh! How depressed and miserable was my soul. At last, I realized that I could no longer lead a double life and no longer serve God and mammon (Matthew 6:24). I had to confess Messiah publicly—whatever the consequences might be. The same day, I resigned as rabbi. The committee members were dismayed. They asked me earnestly not to leave and offered me a higher stipend. Then I witnessed to them frankly of the Messiahship of Yeshua telling them that He is the long-expected Messiah and my personal Redeemer.

Immediately, persecutions followed but they did not intimidate me in anyway. I had expected persecution. I was stoned on the street and had to stay in bed for some time while the doctor came twice a day to attend to and bandage my wounds. When my fellow Jews saw that persecution did not move me, they tried another plan: A prominent Jewish man offered to adopt me as his son and heir provided I would renounce being a believer in Yeshua. I told him: "If you can give me peace for my soul, procure me the presence of God and pardon for my sins, I will renounce Yeshua." He answered: "That I cannot do, for I do not possess myself what you are asking." He never approached me again.

Later, when I was in such danger that I did not know where to turn, I met an American missionary in a Bible shop. He talked to me in Hebrew. When he heard that I had become a believer in Yeshua and was now in danger of my life, he advised me to leave immediately for Beirut in Syria, and gave me a letter of introduction to the Pastor of the Evangelical Church there. I went and two months later was immersed in water according to biblical tradition. Shortly thereafter, I entered a Bible school and after passing the examinations, returned to Palestine in order to work amongst my own people witnessing to them of Yeshua, the Messiah.

My method of work was twofold. First, I showed from passages in the Tanakh that the Lord Yeshua is the true and long predicted Messiah of Israel. I have found more than 200 passages which prove this fact beyond any doubt. Secondly, I showed the superiority of the New Covenant teachings to those of the Talmud. God's blessing rested on this method, and a number of my brethren to whom I have witnessed have come to believe in the Lord Yeshua, the Messiah as their Redeemer.[39]

---

[39] *Note.* From "Rabbis Meet Jesus the Messiah," edited by Sean O'Sullivan, p. 43. Copyright by Messianic Good News. Reprinted with permission.

RABBI DANIEL ZION

Born: Thessalonika, 1883
Died: Haifa, Israel, 1979
Lived and officiated in Sofia, Bulgaria during WWII
Biography by Joseph Shulam followed by autobiographical notes

Rabbi Daniel Zion

After the Balkan War of 1912 many thousands of Jews immigrated into Bulgaria. As the community grew and there was great need for more rabbis. In 1918 a message went from Sofia to Thessalonika (the Jewish cultural hub) to request that rabbis be sent. The head of the Yeshiva in Thessalonika sent his young son, Daniel Solomon Zion to serve the community in Sofia. Rabbi Daniel Zion served the community and was elected to be the chief Rabbi of Bulgaria.[40] Rabbi Daniel Zion's major accomplishment was his activity during the war years.

Rabbi Daniel Zion was invited in the early 1930s to visit Dunnov, who was a teacher of mystic type Christianity. There were three things which Rabbi Daniel Zion appropriated from Dunnov: vegetarianism, getting up early in the morning, starting the day with prayer looking at the sunrise and daily physical

---

[40] See "Two Bulgarian Clergymen Named as Righteous Among the Nations for Saving Jews During the Holocaust," by Yad Vashem, 2001, http://www.yadvashem.org/yv/en/pressroom/pressreleases/pr_details.asp?cid=334, for more information on Rabbi Daniel Zion being the Chief Rabbi at the time of WWII. See also "The History of Bulgaria," by Frederick B. Chary, p. 109, for more information on Rabbi Daniel Zion as Chief Rabbi.

exercise. Dunnov did speak of Yeshua as the Messiah and Savior. He also spoke of the simple lifestyle of the early disciples of Yeshua.

According to Rabbi Daniel Zion, the major change came into his life when, as he was praying looking at the sunrise, a vision of Yeshua appeared to him. He did not know what this vision meant so he asked some of the other rabbis what he should do about it. After the third time that the same vision reappeared, Rabbi Daniel turned toward the figure and spoke to him. The figure was scintillating right out from the sun and the impression that Rabbi Daniel received from this figure is that it spoke back to him identifying himself as Yeshua.

Rabbi Daniel Zion knew that he had to find a source of information that would help him deal with this vision and discern its meaning. At this point Rabbi Daniel went to the patriarchate of the Greek Orthodox Church in Sofia and befriended the Archimandrite Stephen. They developed a close friendship and a frank exchange of ideas on a variety of spiritual subjects including Yeshua and the early church. The Patriarch, who was well versed in the delicate relationship between Jews and Christians, only encouraged the rabbi to forget about Christianity and concentrate on Yeshua himself.

Rabbi Daniel never converted to "Christianity." He started to believe in Yeshua and remained faithful to the Torah keeping lifestyle. A song that Rabbi Daniel wrote about his faith can probably best express his attitude toward Yeshua the Messiah:

No not I, No not I, only you are Yeshua in me!

Only you bring me before the God of my fathers,

Only you can heal me from every evil illness,

No not I, No not I, only you are Yeshua in me!

Only you teach me to love all creation,

Only you teach me to love even the enemy,

No not I, No not I, only you are Yeshua in me!

For this reason I will stay in your love,

For ever will I be within your will,

No not I, No not I, only you are Yeshua in me!

Rabbi Daniel started to collect a very select small group of Jewish people to study the New Covenant each Saturday afternoon in his house. Among these Jews were some of the leading members of the Jewish community in Sofia.

Rabbi Daniel's faith in Yeshua the Messiah became a well known secret in the Jewish community of Bulgaria. However his position was so honored and his services so highly esteemed that none of the Jewish functionaries in Sofia could openly criticize the rabbi. He remained well within the framework of the Jewish community in Bulgaria and did not stop living as an Orthodox Jew in all the rigor of the strictest observance of the Torah and so there was little that his opponents could point to as heresy. However in the background the leadership of the Jewish community started to isolate him slowly.

When Nazi Germany occupied Bulgaria, Rabbi Daniel Zion was the spiritual leader of the Jewish community and became the object of persecution and ridicule. He was taken and publicly flogged in front of the Great Synagogue of Sofia. During these times Rabbi Daniel walked upright before the fascists and his only reaction was to call upon God.[41]

In 1943 the government of Bulgaria made a decision under German pressure to send the Jews outside of Bulgaria. On May 23, Rabbi Daniel Zion gathered all the Jews in the central synagogue of Sofia, which is the second largest synagogue in all of Europe. Every Jew in the city came to the synagogue to pray for the evil decision to be reversed. Rabbi Daniel said publicly to all the community, "It is better for us to die here than in Poland."

When the Jews came out of the synagogue the police attacked the multitude with truncheons and arrested about two hundred and fifty men. The people continued to march toward the Holy Synod and demanded to see the Metropolite Stephen, who was respected by the Jewish community because of his friendly attitude toward them. The Metropolite Stephen promised the Jewish community that he would meet with the King and the ministers and attempt to influence them to change their attitude and stop the persecution of the Jews.

Despite this effort, on May 25, 1943, the expulsion of the Jews from Sofia began. The Commission for Jewish Affairs took from Sofia 10,153 Jews and 3,500 men, and placed them into labour camps in provincial cities. In Sofia remained only 2,300 Jews. The Bulgarian Orthodox Church continued to intercede with the King and the rest of the cabinet for the Jews. The Church was one of the major stumbling blocks in the way of the Bulgarian Government sending the Jews to Auschwitz.

---

[41] Joseph Shulam's family witnessed this event first-hand. He was Rabbi Zion's student and heard personal accounts as well.

The question is asked: Why was the Orthodox Church of Bulgaria so amicable to the Jews? The real reason lay in the special relationship that the Metropolite Stephen and Rabbi Daniel Zion shared with one another.

When there was talk of shipping the Jews to Germany, Rabbi Daniel and his secretary A. A. Anski wrote a letter to the King of Bulgaria. In this letter Rabbi Daniel begged the King in the name of Yeshua not to allow the Jews to be taken out of Bulgaria. Rabbi Daniel wrote in this letter that in a vision that he had seen Yeshua telling him to warn the King from delivering the Jews to the Nazis.[42] After a long ordeal of waiting many hours at the door of the King's palace in Sofia, the rabbi and his secretary were able to deliver this letter to the King's secretary. On the next day the King was going to Germany for a meeting with the Nazi Government and Hitler himself. King Boris of Bulgaria stood his ground and did not submit to the Nazi pressure to deliver the Jews from Bulgaria to the death camps of Poland and Germany.

On the 9th day of September, 1944, the fascist Government of Bulgaria fell and the Communist, under the patronage of Russia. Rabbi Daniel Zion remained the leader and the Chief Rabbi of Bulgaria until 1949 when he, along with most of the Bulgarian Jewish community, immigrated to Israel.

In Israel Rabbi Daniel was immediately accepted as the rabbi of the Bulgarian Jews. When in 1954 Rabbi Samuel Toledano became the Chief Rabbi of Israel, he invited Rabbi Daniel Zion to be a judge in the rabbinical court of Jerusalem. When rumors

---

[42] See "Pet godini pod fashistki gnet," by Rabbi Daniel Tsion, 1945, p. 38-39 and p. 52-53, for Rabbi Daniel Zion's personal messages to the King.

that Rabbi Daniel Zion was a believer in Yeshua started to fly, Rabbi Toledano invited Rabbi Zion to his office to ask him personally about these rumors. Rabbi Daniel explained to Toledano his position. He explained that he accepts Yeshua as the Messiah and he does not accept Christianity as the true expression of the teaching and person of Yeshua the Messiah. Rabbi Toledano said to him that he could live with this position as long as Rabbi Daniel kept it to himself. When Rabbi Daniel said that he did not think that such a message could be kept a secret, Toledano was forced to take Rabbi Daniel to the rabbinic court, and allow the other rabbis to decide what should be done.

In the court, evidence of Rabbi Daniel's faith in Yeshua the Messiah was presented in the form of four books that Rabbi Daniel had written in Bulgarian about Yeshua. The right to speak was given to Rabbi Daniel. Here are the words which Rabbi Daniel Zion spoke in his own defense:

> "I am poor and feeble, persecuted and vulnerable, Yeshua conquered me, and with the New Man he honored me; He delivered me from the poverty-stricken self with his great love, he cherishes me."

> "Every day the canny devil aspires to grab my faith; I hold on to my encourager, and chase the devil away. I stand here alone in my faith; the whole world is against me. I give up all earthly honour for the sake of the Messiah my mate."

The rabbinical court stripped Rabbi Daniel from his rabbinical title, but the Bulgarian Jews continued to honour Rabbi Daniel as their rabbi. A Russian Jew who was one of the early Zionist settlers in Rishon LeZion, and had become a believer in Yeshua, had given Rabbi Daniel Zion a building on Yeffet Street in the heart of Jaffa for a Synagogue. In that Synagogue Rabbi Daniel officiated until the 6th of October, 1973. In this Synagogue Rabbi Daniel Zion did not often speak of Yeshua openly, but many times he brought stories and parables from the New Covenant. However, each Sabbath after the Synagogue Rabbi Daniel would bring home a group of his fellow worshipers from the Synagogue and they would study about Yeshua and from the New Testament all the Sabbath afternoon until they would go back to the Synagogue to say the evening prayers.

Rabbi Daniel Zion wrote hundreds of songs about Yeshua the Messiah, Sabbath and the good life. He also wrote books on the subject of vegetarianism, health food, and natural living. Yeshua was his savior and friend and until the last days of his life Rabbi Daniel Zion lived up to the poem that he wrote with the acrostic of his name, Daniel Zion (דניאל ציון) the Servant of God.

The (Daver) Word of God is my path,

The (Ner) Lamp of God is my guide,

The (Iraat) Fear of God is the beginning of Wisdom,

The (Ahavat) Love of God is my Life,

The (Laasoth) Doing the will of God is my aspiration,

(Zedek) Righteousness and Justice are my goals,

His (Isurim) Suffering is my atonement,

He will (OYagen) protect you in all your ways,

The (Nezah) Eternal one of Israel is my comfort.

In 1979 Rabbi Daniel Zion departed to be with the Lord in a ripe old age of 96 years. The Bulgarian Jewish community of Israel gave him full military, and state honours. His bier stood in the center of Jaffa with a military guard and at noon was carried by men all the way to the Holon cemetery on foot. He was buried as the Chief Rabbi of Bulgarian Jews who saved them from the Nazi holocaust. He was 100 per cent Jewish and 100 per cent a follower and disciple of Yeshua the Messiah.[43]

PERSONAL ADDRESSES & WRITINGS

TESTIMONY ON ISRAEL RADIO "KOL ISRAEL"
September 14, 1952

Rabbi Zion was allowed to tell of his experience on "Kol Yisrael" (The Voice of Israel), the official broadcasting station in Israel. Such a thing had never been permitted before. The following is part of a transcript of his radio address:[44]

"More than twenty years ago, I had the first opportunity of reading the New Covenant. It influenced me greatly. I began to speak about it in a small circle in Bulgaria. I always regretted that Yeshua the Messiah has been estranged from the community of Israel. Yeshua the Messiah did nothing but good for the Jewish people. He called them to repentance, proclaimed the Kingdom of God and Divine Love, a love towards all men, even one's

---

[43] *Note.* "Rabbi Daniel Zion: The Chief Rabbi of Bulgarian Jews during World War II," by Joseph Shulam. Copyright by Netivyah Bible Instruction Ministry. Reprinted with permission.
[44] Introduction written by Jacob Gartenhaus, the director of IBJM and personal acquaintance.

enemies. To our great regret we have had to pay a heavy price for the sin of rejecting the true Messiah. But I must confess that my position as a rabbi did not allow me at once to come out openly before the world in order to declare this truth, until God, in His great mercy, set me free from all fear. He brought me into this country of Israel, where at first I discharged my duties as a rabbi of Jaffa."

"After I gave up my position (as Chief Rabbi of Jaffa, Israel), I went to Jerusalem, where for a whole month I engaged in fasting, prayer and supplication. It was then that I asked God to show me the right way, and the eternal God heard my prayer. On the first of Shevat, 5710 (January/February, 1950), the Holy Spirit revealed to me that Yeshua is indeed the true Messiah, who suffered for us and sacrificed Himself for our sin. A burning fire in my heart gave me no rest until I had publicly confessed my faith in the blood atonement of the True and living God, the Lord Yeshua the Messiah, the one and only Messiah of Israel."

"In spite of all the difficulties, suffering and persecutions, which I have endured incessantly, nothing could dissuade me from my faith. On the contrary, God to whom I had given my heart and to whom I turn in all my needs, has given me the strength and power to continue my witness. He spoke to me through a verse in (the word of God), Isaiah 41:10: *"Fear not, for I am with you; Be not dismayed, for I am your God. I will strengthen you, Yes, I will help you, I will uphold you with My righteous right hand."* By this I understood that a great and important task has been given to me by the Eternal God, which I must accomplish at all costs. Do not think that I have left Judaism. On the contrary, I have remained Jewish, and have become more Jewish because Yeshua Himself remained Jewish.

MESSAGE TO JEWISH RABBIS

The following is taken from a message given by Rabbi Daniel Zion to his colleagues, the rabbis of Israel, before whom he was tried:

"I know that according to your knowledge and ideas I go a wrong way, when I accept Yeshua as the Messiah and Redeemer. Before the witness stand of Heaven I told you that I prayed to the Lord with tears and fasting for many years that He should lead me in the path of righteousness, that I should do His will only, not my own. I spoke to you about the wonderful way in which He revealed Himself to me, not once only, but many times. You replied that all this was imagination and illusion. Forgive me, please, when I say that the imagination is with you, gentlemen, and the true and real things appear as illusion to you."

"I know that the narrow-minded education and the high offices of the rabbis are a veil, hiding the truth from them. You can no longer judge objectively. I, too, suffered from it, but God in His grace has shown me, by the Holy Spirit, the straight path, in spite of my sins. By Him I have been guided for years and He leads me on the path of righteousness. Therefore, I tell you, even if I were the only one to believe in Yeshua as the Messiah, I would not consider that to be an imagination; but now I see that millions of men acknowledge Him, among them thousands of highly educated Jews. Some rabbis too, believe in Yeshua as the Messiah. Have they fallen prey to imagination and deception?"

"If you rabbis would pray to God with your whole heart and read the New Covenant thoughtfully, approaching this book and the Messiah Yeshua with reverence, I am convinced that God would open your eyes."

"Yeshua did nothing but good; He called Israel to repentance and to the Kingdom of God. He did many signs and wonders, as no prophet before Him. He wished to unite people; that they should love each other and also their enemies. Thus He wished to build a bridge between Israel and the nations; there should be peace between them and the prophecies of Isaiah and all the prophets be fulfilled, that the Lord would be King over all the earth."

"The truth must be spoken. Our fathers committed a grave sin, when they condemned to death Him who was without sin. Our fathers sinned and perished. We suffered for their crime. Do we wish to continue to suffer?"

"We must bring restitution for the wrong. We must receive Yeshua as Jew and Messiah of God. He lived among the Jews and sacrificed Himself for the Jews, to make atonement for their sins with His blood. He is risen and will come again to redeem us with a perfect redemption."

"As a messenger of God, I was to give warning. First, there is the warning, and then the chastisement follows.

By this will you know that the Lord has sent me; and that the words I speak are not my own. The days of visitation have come—the days of retribution! If you receive Yeshua as the true Messiah, He will redeem us a second time with perfect redemption. If not, much suffering will come upon the people of Israel."

"And to you, rabbis, be it said: '*Mene, Mene, Tekel Upharsin (Weighed in the balances and found wanting)*!'" (Daniel 5:25).[45]

---

[45] *Note.* From "Rabbi Zion's Message on the Voice of Israel Radio 1952" and "Message to the Rabbis," by Dr. Jacob Gartenhaus, 1978, *The Remarkable Conversion of a Chief Rabbi.* Copyright by IBJM. Reprinted with permission.

Map of Yugoslavia

RABBI ASHER LEVY

*Born: Yugoslavia
Autobiography*

RABBI ASHER LEVY

I was a rabbi for thirty-five years. Born in Yugoslavia, I was brought up in a very orthodox Jewish home. I was taught to say formal prayers and wear phylacteries as prescribed for every pious Jew (Deut. 6:8; 11:18).

At the age of fifteen, I went to the theological school for rabbis where I studied the Tanakh and Talmudic commentaries. Six years later I was ordained as rabbi in Romania. Afterwards, I served in Belgium, England and California.

Outwardly, I was happy and successful in my ministry but in my heart I was restless and discontented because I suffered much as a result of the emptiness of life in general. Six years ago, I met a Jewish man with whom I discussed this matter.

I did not know that he was a believer in Yeshua, the Messiah. His advice was "Read Isaiah 53." I then read this well-known chapter concerning Yeshua of Nazareth, which says that "*He was wounded for our transgressions, he was bruised for our iniquities.*" I felt urged further to examine the Hebrew Scriptures and found these words written by the same prophet:

> For unto us a child is born, unto us a son is given; and the government shall be upon his shoulders; and his name shall be called Wonderful, Counsellor, The mighty God, The everlasting Father, The Prince of Peace. Of the increase of his government and peace there shall be no end, upon the throne of David, and upon his kingdom, to order it, and to establish it with judgment and with justice from henceforth even for ever. The zeal of the Lord of hosts will perform this (Isaiah 9:6-7).

I also read:

> "Hear ye now, O house of David; is it a small thing for you to weary men, but will ye weary my God also? Therefore the Lord himself shall give you a sign; behold a virgin shall conceive, and bear a son, and shall call his name 'Immanuel' (God with us)" (Isaiah 7:13-14).

This proved to me that Yeshua was and is the Messiah in whom all the prophecies were fulfilled. Meanwhile, I had found a clear portrait of the Messiah in a small book (the New Covenant) which I had the privilege of getting into my hands. It was my first introduction to the New Covenant. I started reading it like any other book, from the beginning: "*The book of the generation of Yeshua, the Messiah, the son of David, the son of Abraham*" and found to my amazement that I was reading a *Jewish* book about a *Jew*. By reading it carefully, I came to the conclusion that Yeshua, the Messiah was a Jew of the race of Abraham and David; that He was born of a Jewish virgin in the Jewish town of Bethlehem; of a Jewish tribe, the tribe of Judah. Because He knew the Law and the Prophets, I followed Him on His journeys through the Holy Land, listened to His beautiful sayings and teachings, observed and admired His compassion and healings. It became my spiritual food. His promise of forgiveness of sins and eternal life to those who believe in Him, drew me until I trusted Him as my Messiah and my personal Saviour.

I want to confirm the fact that my heart does not condemn me for my new belief, because I feel that I am still a Jew and shall always be a Jew. I have not renounced our inheritance of Abraham, Isaac and Jacob. Like Rabbi Shaul of Tarsus I can say after my acceptance of Messiah as my Saviour: *"Are they Hebrews? So am I. Are they Israelites? So am I. Are they the seed of Abraham? So am I"* (2 Cor.11:22). Thus, I repeat with pride the word of Romans 1:16: *"For I am not ashamed of the Good News of Messiah; for it is the power of God unto salvation to everyone that believeth; to the Jew first and also to the Greek."*

The brilliant example of the great apostle, Rabbi Shaul influenced me very much, and gave me the courage to accept the Lord Yeshua as my personal Saviour. Rabbi Shaul first was a zealous persecutor of Messiah, and then became His most faithful follower. He was a disciple of that great doctor of the Law, Raban Gamaliel, at whose feet he sat. It is believed that Raban Gamaliel became a follower of Messiah before Rabbi Shaul did. The Scriptures tell us that some wanted to kill Peter and the other apostles because they were preaching Messiah so boldly.

Then one in the council stood up, a Pharisee named Gamaliel, a teacher of the law held in respect by all the people, and commanded them to put the apostles outside for a little while. And he said to them: "Men of Israel, take heed to yourselves what you intend to do regarding these men. And now I say to you, keep away from these men and let them alone; for if this plan or this work is of men, it will come to nothing; but if it is of God you cannot overthrow it; lest you even be found to fight against God" (Acts 5:34-35; 38-39).

It is two thousand years since the lowly Galilean, Yeshua, traversed the hills and dales of Palestine, and He is still Master of the world. His Good News is still preached, and Yeshua's name as the Messiah of Israel is still proclaimed. And His message is still repeated everywhere: *"For God so loved the world, that He gave His only begotten Son, that whosoever believeth in Him should not perish but have everlasting life"* (John 3:16).

- Hear, O Israel[46]

---

[46] *Note.* From "Rabbis Meet Jesus the Messiah," edited by Sean O'Sullivan, p. 33-34. Copyright by Messianic Good News. Reprinted with permission.

RABBI MAX WERTHEIMER

Born: Baden, Germany, 1863
Died: Ada, Ohio, 1941
Smikha: Hebrew Union College, 1889

RABBI MAX WERTHEIMER

Born of orthodox Jewish parents, my earliest childhood impression was of my parents rising in the morning very early in order to spend a long time reading the Hebrew prayers. Even in the cold winter, before fires were kindled for their physical comfort, they carried on faithfully these early devotions. In so far as their knowledge of God was concerned, they were a devout and God-fearing couple.

From the age of five to fifteen my training was in a Jewish school, in Orthodox Judaism. A scholarly Jewish man instructed me in the five books of Moses. I went to the Gymnasium for my classical training and later was apprenticed to a manufacturer, doing office work. My associates at that time led me into the sinful pleasures of the world, and although I attended synagogue and read my Hebrew prayers on the Sabbath, I drifted from the faith of my fathers.

A parental decision to send me to America to pursue my classical education brought me to Hebrew Union College in Cincinnati, Ohio. I graduated in seven years, having meanwhile taken my degrees in letters and Hebrew literature, and four years later my Master's degree. We studied the Tanakh, translated it from Hebrew into the vernacular, went through Jewish history from the beginning to the present day, and learned the oral laws.

After finishing the rabbinical course we were publicly ordained and inducted into the rabbinical office. My first call was to Dayton, Ohio, where I officiated as Rabbi for ten years, during which I made many friends and received many tokens of love, which I treasure highly. In my Friday evening lectures I spoke on social, industrial and economic questions, monotheism, ethical culture, the moral systems of the Jews, etc. In the Saturday morning addresses I took weekly sections of the Pentateuch, followed by a corresponding section of the prophets. On Sunday, I taught Sunday School from eight in the morning until five in the evening, with one hour intermission for dinner.

In 1895 a series of meetings was held in the Christian Church of Dayton, with various denominational pastors giving addresses on their religion. I stood proudly before that audience of professing Christians and told them why I was a Jew and would not believe in their Christ as my Messiah and Saviour. In the audience sat a humble aged woman, a devout Christian, who was deeply stirred as she listened. "O God," she prayed, "bring Dr. Wertheimer to realize his utter need of that Saviour he so boastingly rejects. Bring him if necessary, to the very depths in order that he may know his need of my Lord Yeshua the Messiah."

What unforeseen forces were brought into action, as a result of that unknown woman's heart cry! How perfectly satisfied with life I was that day: I had a young, attractive, accomplished wife, was Rabbi of the B'nai Yeshorum Synagogue, had a beautiful home, a comfortable income, a place of prominence in the community, had become an honorary member of the Ministerial Association, was a member of the Present-Day Club, served as chaplain in the Masonic lodge, and was a popular speaker before women's clubs, schools, civic organizations, etc. Had you visited my library at the time you would have found a wide range of reading. I had every book Bob Ingersoll wrote, read them, and corresponded with the author. I was an oft-invited guest speaker in every denominational church in the city. I was satisfied with life! My wife and I enjoyed the musical treats; we had a large home, two servants, and a beautiful baby boy and daughter, Rose.

Suddenly there came a change! My wife was taken seriously ill, and in spite of many physicians and specialists, she died, leaving me a distraught widower with two little children. After the funeral, I put Rose in the care of my mother-in-law, advertised for a housekeeper for myself and the boy, and found myself the most miserable of men. I could not sleep. I walked the streets, striving to forget the void, the vacancy in my heart and life. My dreams of a successful career and serene domestic life were all shattered. Where was comfort to be found? The heavens were brass when I called on the God of my fathers! How could I, as a rabbi speak words of comfort to others when my own sorrow had brought me to despair. I investigated Spiritism, but found it utter fallacy. My experience was comparable to Job's when he cried: *"My days are swifter than a weaver's shuttle, and are spent without hope"* (Job 7:6).

The tenth year of my rabbinical office drew to its close. I decided not to accept re-election, and resigned. I wanted to think over things! I would study. Where is the spirit and soul of one who was such a gifted pianist, who gave charm to life; who made existence so sweet? What had become of all the faculties, the intents and purposes of that active, keen mind?

I attended meetings and read the literature of Theosophy and Christian Science, only to find it futile and hopeless.[47] One night as I returned home down-hearted, melancholy, and perplexed, I went to my room, locked the door, and went down on my knees. As I was down on the floor, crushed, a failure, two thoughts came to my mind: the holiness of God, and my own wretched and discordant condition. Often in the Temple I had preached on the holiness of God and the wretchedness of somebody else; but this time it gripped me. Mind you, I saw no vision; I heard no voice. The thoughts came this way: "How can I, wretched as I am, ever stand before that God Who is so Holy, before Whom sinless angels have to veil their faces?"

As I was meditating on this, a scene from the Tanakh came to my mind. I saw no vision, I heard no voice. This was the scene: When the Children of Israel were in Egypt as slaves, plague upon plague came upon Egypt, and yet Israel remained in slavery until God said to Moses:

> "Moses, tell every family to take a lamb without blemish, without spot, and kill that lamb—shed the blood of that lamb and sprinkle it upon the door posts of the house, the two side posts and on the upper door post. I will pass through Egypt this night to judge Egypt and its gods, but when I see the blood I will pass over you."

---

[47] *Note.* From "How a Rabbi Found Peace: Personal Testimony of Dr. Max Wertheimer," by Dr. Max Wertheimer. Copyright by Wertheimer Publications.

I said to myself, "Then this is the way the Children of Israel got out of Egypt. God makes something of the blood."

A second scene from the Tanakh came to my mind. The judicial laws, including the Ten Commandments, are declared in Exodus twenty to twenty-three, but, there was no covenant relationship established between the holy יהוה and Israel until God said to Moses, *"Take oxen and bring them as burnt-offerings to the Lord,"* as you find recorded in Exodus twenty-four. He was commanded to kill these oxen and take the blood of the oxen in two big basins; one basin of blood he sprinkled upon the temporarily constructed altar and the twelve pillars of stone, and the other basin of blood he sprinkled upon the people in front of him and upon the document or scroll, which he held in his own hand. When the sprinkling of the blood was over, God entered thus into covenant relationship with Israel. I said to myself, "God makes something of the blood."

While still in meditation, a third scene from the Tanakh came to my mind. I heard no voice; I saw no vision. This was of the High Priest entering the Holy of Holies on the Day of Atonement. "How did he enter?" I wondered. "Did he take a Turkish bath, a Russian bath, and anoint himself with aromatic perfumes? Did he bring with him a beautiful bouquet to offer to God?" No. If he had entered the Holy of Holies that way he would have been a dead man; that isn't the way to come into God's presence. No, sir. He had to bring the blood of his own substitutionary sin-offering from a ceremonially clean bullock . . . and that blood he brought into the Holy Place and sprinkled it on the veil that separated the sanctuary from the Holy of Holies. Then, and not until then, was he allowed to lift the veil that separated the Holy Place from the Most Holy Place. He took that blood and sprinkled it in the Holiest of Holies on the east of the Mercy Seat once and seven times before it. Upon the sprinkling of the blood upon the Mercy Seat came the voice of יהוה *"I have pardoned thee according to thy word,"* and I said, "God makes something of the blood."

Then, there came an impression to me that I tried to dispel from my mind. It was Calvary's Cross. The reason I tried to shut my mind to it was because of my Jewish prejudices against the Cross. Due to my Jewish upbringing I had no use for the sacrifice of the cross to begin with. When I came into Christian Science I believed on Yeshua the Messiah as the greatest Prophet of Israel, as the Great Way shower, but not as the only begotten Son of God Who came into this world to pay the penalty of the sin of the world by the shedding of His sinless blood. Consequently I thought to myself, "To believe in Him Who hung on that Cross would be contrary to the Word of God as recorded in Jeremiah 17:5 where it states: *'Cursed be the man that trusteth in man.'"* I considered the One Who hung on the Cross as a mere man, not as the God-appointed Sacrifice for sin (John 3:16). So I reasoned that to believe in Him I would be under a curse. [48]

I studied about Judaism but it answered no questions, satisfied no craving of my heart. Then I began reading the New Covenant and comparing it with the Tanakh. Many passages were read, pondered, meditated upon. One made a definite impression: the fifty-third chapter of Isaiah, eleventh verse, last clause. *"By His knowledge shall My righteous servant justify many, for He shall bear their iniquities."* Here was the only mention of that phrase, "My righteous servant," I could find. It is found nowhere else in

---

[48] *Note.* From "Rabbinism to Christ: The Story of My Life," by Dr. Max Wertheimer, 1934. Copyright 1934 by Wertheimer Publications.

the Word of God in either Covenant. We have "David, my servant," "Isaiah, my servant," "Daniel, my servant," but here it is: "My *righteous* servant." I said to myself: "Who is that righteous servant? To whom does the prophet refer?" I argued: "Whoever that 'righteous servant' of יהוה is, of one thing I am sure: he is not Israel, because the prophet declares Israel to be a sinful nation, a people laden with iniquity, a leprous nation. The righteous servant of יהוה must be One Who is holy. If it isn't Israel, who could it be?" I decided it must be Isaiah. But in Isaiah 6 I found it could never be the prophet for he confesses himself to be a guilty sinner and a man of unclean lips in God's sight. "My righteous servant." Who could it be? Then I began to study the context of the fifty-third chapter and in Isaiah 50:6 I found, *"I gave My back to the smiters."* I pondered that: Who gave his back to the smiters? In the beginning of the chapter it says: "Thus saith יהוה." יהוה is the only speaker in the chapter. יהוה gave His back to the smiters? Had God a back? When and why was it smitten? Who smote it? Further I read: "Who gave His cheeks to them that plucked off the hair." And still further: "I hid not My face from shame and spitting." What did all this mean? Who had been so abused? When? Why? Did יהוה have all these human characteristics? I studied more and more various prophetic utterances. In Psalm 110:1 it is written: *"The Lord said to my Lord, Sit Thou at My right hand until I make Thine enemies Thy footstool."* Here was David himself, speaking of his own seed and calling Him "Lord." How did He get up there? Why didn't God specify? Why didn't He speak so plainly to Israel that every Jew could understand?

In confusion I decided to begin at the first chapter of Isaiah and read the book through. I was stopped at the ninth: *"For unto us a child is born, unto us a son is given, and the government shall be upon his shoulders; His name shall be called Wonderful, Counsellor, the Mighty God, the Everlasting Father, the Prince of Peace."* Here was a most incomprehensible thing!

I was faced with the doctrine of the Trinity. We Jews have a popular monotheistic slogan: *"Shema Yisroel, Adonai, Elohenu, Adonai, Echad."* The word "echad" means *one*. Upon that word the doctrine of unity of יהוה is rooted and grounded, the entire philosophy of Judaism is based. Taught by the Rabbis for ages, that word "echad" means absolute unity. Now I could not believe it; my teaching was wrong! I began to study the word, and I discovered it meant, not *absolute* unity, but *composite* unity. Let me illustrate: Adam and Eve became one flesh; the Hebrew for one flesh is *bosor echad,* a composite unity. Moses sent twelve spies into Canaan, and they returned bearing a gigantic bunch of grapes. That cluster of grapes is called in Hebrew *eschol-echad.* With hundreds of grapes on the stem it could not have been an absolute unity; they are called in Hebrew "one cluster." Composite unity. There was wickedness committed in Gibeah of Benjamin which disgraced יהוה and His name and character. The other tribes were indignant and *"all the people arose as one man."* That is what I want you to see: at that time the men of Israel, beside Benjamin, were 400,000 men of war, yet they were *"knit together as one man."* (In Hebrew: *Ish Echad.)* Here again composite unity: thousands acted as one! These and other Scriptures showed conclusively that *echad* cannot be an absolute unity.

But another question troubled me: if He Who was on the cross was truly an incarnation of יהוה, then who was in Heaven? I turned to the eighteenth of Genesis. Abraham had three visitors:

two angels and the third he addressed fourteen times as יהוה. Later two went away, but the third said to Abraham:

"Shall I hide from Abraham that which I shall do? I am going down to Sodom and Gomorrah to see whether or not they have done altogether according to the report which has come to Me. If not I will know whether to destroy the cities."

Abraham interceded for them, the Lord went His way, and Abraham went home. Now here is the point: We find יהוה inspecting the moral condition of Sodom and Gomorrah and refusing to spare them because not even ten righteous citizens could be found within their borders. But in this same chapter we have this statement: "Then יהוה rained upon Sodom and upon Gomorrah brimstone and fire from יהוה out of Heaven." How and why could there be two יהוה, one walking the streets of Sodom and another in heavenly places? It must be one omnipresent יהוה! Then if that were true, He could be simultaneously both in Heaven and with and in Yeshua on the cross.

I could hold out in unbelief no longer; I was convinced of the truth of God as it is in Yeshua the Messiah. I cried: "Lord, I believe that Thou as יהוה Yeshua hast made the atonement for me. I believe that יהוה Yeshua died for me! I believe Thou has the ability and power! From henceforth I will publicly confess Yeshua as my Saviour and Lord!" Thus after months of searching I was convinced that Yeshua was the righteous servant of יהוה (יהוה - צדקנו) "The Lord our righteousness!"

On March 30, 1904, I publicly confessed Yeshua the Messiah in the Central Baptist Church and having been licensed to preach, doors readily opened to me.

115

I started out in Bible teaching and God was ever faithful: Were I to write of all the manifestations of His goodness and grace, it would fill a book. Critical operations, publication of my books, supplying all our needs, He never failed to care and provide. In Messiah I have found my only abiding comfort for every sorrow.

As a rabbi, I had yearned to give the bereaved some hope on which to lean, but how could I give that which I did not possess? I gave sympathy, but in times of heart aching grief and tragedy, sympathy is of little comfort. But to the heartbroken how satisfying and glorious are the words of our Lord Yeshua the Messiah: *"I am the resurrection and the life: he that believeth in Me, though he were dead, yet shall he live; and whosoever liveth and believeth in Me shall never die."* And again: *"Verily, verily I say unto you: He that heareth My Word, and believeth on Him that sent Me, hath (possesses now) everlasting life and shall not come into condemnation, but is passed from death unto life."*

There is but one eternal life. There is but one source of eternal life; that is God's Son. What a great and glorious message we, His redeemed ones, are commissioned to deliver today. [49]

---

[49] *Note.* From "How a Rabbi Found Peace: Personal Testimony of Dr. Max Wertheimer," by Dr. Max Wertheimer. Copyright 1934 by Wertheimer Publications.

View of the Jewish district (Mellah) at Fez from its ethnic cemetery, Morocco.

RABBI AZRIEL BEN ISAAC

Born: Morocco, 1940
Autobiography

RABBI AZRIEL BEN ISAAC

I was born in Morocco in 1940, into a very religious and observant family, of rabbinical descent. My father was a rabbi in Casablanca, and in 1941 he died of a severe illness. As there were eleven children, and all small, the economic situation worsened as time went on. My mother decided to send some of her children to adoptive families. After I reached three years of age, she sent me also to a family for adoption. The father was a rabbi who succeeded my father. After a year and a half, this man also died and I was transferred to another family, in the town of Saffi, one hundred kilometres from Casablanca.

In this new family, I lived until I was seven years old, when they sent me to Meknes, where there was an orphanage. There I was taken care of and taught in a yeshiva until I was thirteen. Then I went to another town, Masagan, where there was a bigger yeshiva for boys of thirteen to eighteen years of age. I studied until I was sixteen and a half, when I emigrated to Israel, straight into a yeshiva at Bnei Brak, up to the age of eighteen. I was then conscripted into the Army until I was twenty-one, in 1961.

After demobilization, I requested the Jewish Agency to grant me living quarters in a town in the North, where I am now, because one of my sisters was living here. I then entered the building trade, while in the evenings I was with the local rabbinate, working as a teacher in a yeshiva. In 1962 I married and in 1965 was given a job at the local post office, which suited me well, because I could finish at about eleven in the morning. This enabled me to travel to a small town not far from home, where there was a big yeshiva for rabbis. There I underwent higher Talmudic studies, until 1980, when the yeshiva closed because of political friction between the local council and the rabbinical heads of this institution. However, I obtained rabbinical status and a diploma to be a shokhet (a Kosher butcher), and a diploma to teach the Scriptures and Talmud.

Today, I am the father of six children: four grown-up daughters and two younger sons. Three of my daughters have completed army service and two have married: one has two children, and the other has one. The rest of my children live at home.

Dear brethren, what I have told you is a brief and very simple summary; but in reality it was not so simple, for if I had told all my past in detail, it would have taken a book to write. Therefore I shall make do with the above short account; because, until I arrived at this point, I went through a lot of troubles, shifting from family to family, place to place, from town to town, and from country to country. For the moment, this is not important. What does matter is my life in the Messiah; how, through all this, after all my life, when I went through many yeshivas and much Torah learning, I came to faith in Yeshua the Messiah.

Never did I believe in Him, all the time claiming that this was a false Messiah who brought only trouble to all our generations.

At times, when I would meet a messianic believer, a very difficult situation would arise, full of arguments, when I would deny Yeshua and would stand only on my beliefs, explaining to them that Yeshua could not be the Messiah since He was put to death by others.

In short, never did I imagine or believe that the day would come when I would turn into a believer in Yeshua, faithful to the Messiah; that my heart would burn with a desire to be a true proclaimer of the Messiah, Yeshua, especially to the Jews everywhere in North Africa. I sincerely hope that, by God's help, I shall succeed in fulfilling this holy, messianic task, to which I look forward so much, with all my heart.

I am very happy to declare that my heart and conscience do not trouble me nor do they condemn me over my faith in Yeshua, because I am still a Jew and will always remain a Jew. I have not denied the faith of Abraham, Isaac and Jacob.

As Rabbi Shaul of Tarsus said, so say I (with the receiving of Yeshua into my life as Redeemer and Saviour) as is written in 2 Corinthians 11:22: *"Are they Hebrews? So am I. Are they Israelites? So am I. Are they the seed of Abraham? So am I."*

Therefore I too can certainly concur with the words of Rabbi Shaul, in Romans 1:16: *"I am not ashamed of the Good News of Messiah for it is the power of God unto salvation to everyone that believes, to the Jew first and also to the Gentile."* This verse of the mighty apostle Shaul influenced me deeply and gave me the courage to receive the Lord Yeshua as my personal Saviour.

In sincere religious zeal, Shaul first persecuted, both Messiah and His disciples but then became Yeshua's most faithful and dedicated disciple. In the same way, I now really wish to believe in the Messiah Yeshua and to live like Rabbi Shaul amongst all the Jews of North Africa.[50]

---

[50] *Note.* From "Rabbis Meet Jesus the Messiah," edited by Sean O'Sullivan, p. 78-80. Copyright by Messianic Good News. Reprinted with permission.

Cupola of the Neue Synagogue, Berlin. Built between 1859–1866 as the main Synagogue of Berlin.

RABBI GEORGE BENEDICT

Born: Spandau in Berlin, Germany, circa 1880
Emigrated to the United States, 1905

RABBI GEORGE BENEDICT

George Benedict was born in Germany where his father was a rabbi. When the rabbi accepted a call to Sheffield the family emigrated to England. There, young Benedict attended school. It was his desire to serve the God of his fathers by becoming a rabbi. Immediately after his Bar Mitzvah, he applied for admission to the rabbinical seminary in London. The Chief Rabbi, Dr. H. Adler, advised him, however, to wait two or three years, but Benedict begged to be admitted as a student though he was so young. Eventually, Dr. Adler consented to admit the boy to the seminary. Benedict was overwhelmed with joy. In his imagination he already saw the fulfillment of his dream of becoming a rabbi and walking in the footsteps of his father.

First Acquaintance With The Gospel

During his years of study in the big city of London, the rabbinical student visited not only many synagogues but also evangelical churches. A sermon on the temptation of Yeshua made such an impression on him that he decided to read the New Covenant, until then an unknown book to him.

In Farrington Street, he came across a barrow with books and bought the "Holy Book of the Christians;" hiding it under his coat, he took it to his room. In his biography he says:

> I shall never forget the verse I read when I opened the New Covenant. I felt compelled to read it again and again. These are the words: *"These things I have spoken unto you, that in me ye might have peace. In the world ye shall have tribulation: but be of good cheer; I have overcome the world"* (John 16:33). I fell on my knees and for a long time meditated on these wonderful words. On the point of going to a gruesome death, Yeshua could say: *"I have overcome the world."*

Benedict Dares To Speak Up For Yeshua

Though at that time Benedict had not yet come to a living faith in Yeshua—but had only admired and honoured the noble character of the Nazarene from afar—he was courageous enough to state his conviction in a written test. The subject he had voluntarily chosen was "Yeshua: a picture of Jewry." He quoted Isaiah 9:2, *"The people who walked in darkness have seen a great light."* He described the human sublimity of Yeshua and emphasized that He was Israel's greatest son. The principal of the seminary was startled when he read the essay. Benedict had to appear before the council of lecturers who questioned him on his attitude towards Christianity. They reproached him for having visited churches. The young student declared his opinions frankly and quoted Jewish writings in his support. The lecturers then decided to discuss amongst themselves whether Benedict could remain as a student. It was hard for him to await the decision. He took his Hebrew Bible and read again Isaiah 9:2,

"The people who walked in darkness have seen a great light" and then he came to these words in verse 6, *"For unto us a child is born, unto us a son is given: and the government shall be upon his shoulder: and his name shall be called Wonderful, Counselor, the Mighty God, the Everlasting Father, the Prince of Peace."* Benedict asked himself: "Of whom did the great prophet Isaiah speak in this verse, seven hundred years before the birth of Yeshua? Did he speak of Yeshua? A small minority of our people are still waiting for the Messiah, but the vast majority are not concerned about this matter. One-third of the world recognizes Yeshua who was born of our nation. What blindness, what folly not to accept Him as our Saviour!"

Benedict In America

To his great surprise the council allowed him to remain in the seminary. He was merely warned. After he had finished his studies, Benedict left for the U.S.A. where he was appointed rabbi in one of the southern states. Soon he became known as a writer far beyond the confines of his own congregation. The attention of the Christian church was also attracted, especially by his courageous plea for the Korean Christians, who at that time were oppressed by the Japanese. In the scattered communities of Korean Christians with whom he had come into contact during his lecture tours, he had become acquainted with genuine Christianity. Though many Jewish people disapproved of his lectures in the interest of the Korean Christians, the young rabbi remained steadfast. [51]

---

[51] *Note.* From "Rabbis Meet Jesus the Messiah," edited by Sean O'Sullivan, p. 48. Copyright by Messianic Good News. Reprinted with permission.

When questioned about his faith he said: "But I am not a Christian, but, on the contrary, a Jewish rabbi, and I am doing what I do for Korea's sake, for humanity, not for Christianity."[52]

Although Rabbi Benedict had a certain level of faith that Yeshua was the Messiah from his previous reading, he in no way considered himself His follower. While visiting many churches he was at the same time drawn towards Yeshua and repulsed.[53] He wrote,

I know that at night time when I would recall the day's work I would often wonder what the veil was made of which hid from me the Messiah preached through simple Korean lives, ignorantly yet eloquently. What was the material of the veil, if it existed, I longed to know, and which sometimes, not without anguish and deepest yearning, I wished might be rent from me?[54]

The Rabbi Becomes A Dedicated Believer In Yeshua

At a conference in aid of the oppressed Koreans, Benedict was asked to speak in a church in Philadelphia. After the church service the congregation commemorated the Lord's death as He had commanded. Benedict had never before been present at a Communion service (called the Passover of the New Covenant in many Messianic congregations). It reminded him of certain Jewish ceremonies such as the Passover. Softly the minister asked him if he would like to partake. For a moment the rabbi

---

[52] *Note.* From "Christ Finds a Rabbi: An Autobiography," by Rabbi George Benedict, 1932, p. 142. Copyright 1932 by George Benedict.
[53] *Note* from the editor. See Rabbi Benedict's autobiography for more details.
[54] *Note.* From "Christ Finds a Rabbi: An Autobiography," by Rabbi George Benedict, 1932, p. 147. Copyright 1932 by George Benedict.

hesitated, thinking: "Is Holy Communion not for Christians only? And I am a Jew." But when the minister quoted the words of Yeshua, *"Do this in remembrance of Me,"* all doubt and hesitation disappeared. Rabbi Benedict took the bread, and later the wine, in remembrance of the death of Yeshua who had laid down His life also for the sin of Israel.[55]

The Rabbi Continues In His Faith

Rabbi George Benedict continued in his faith in the Messiah throughout the rest of his life. In 1935 he published his autobiography, "Messiah Finds a Rabbi," in which he poetically describes how God worked throughout his life:

And imperceptibly the current of Messiah has deepened and widened within me until, from the narrow stream in child life, it is now keeping all my life afloat, and bearing it onward, where I do not know, but confidently assured that God does.

He, who as Key Warden, opened the door of my tomb in my youth, has a key for every tomb. And, alas, many are the souls, as was mine, that are buried and struggling to free themselves and cannot get out.

He has a key for every tomb.

He has a key for you, and you, and you.

I am pointing to a host of non-believers, of every creed and no creed, of every colour, tribe, and nation.

---

[55] *Note.* From "Rabbis Meet Jesus the Messiah," edited by Sean O'Sullivan, p. 49. Copyright by Messianic Good News. Reprinted with permission.

For you He carries the master key, the universal key of life.

Yes, you, whoever and wherever you are, raise but your face in His direction; look Him in the eyes as I did, and you will feel something in your heart where the lock is. It is the key of Yeshua opening the door to let in peace and contentment and joy abundant.

Ask. He will release your captive soul.

Call. You will be free.

I speak from experience. For who opened the door of my tomb?

Yeshua! He had the key, and used the key.

Who else? For whence have I this life?[56]

---

[56] *Note.* From "Christ Finds a Rabbi: An Autobiography," by Rabbi George Benedict, 1932, p. 396-397. Copyright 1932 by George Benedict.

RABBI ISIDOR ZWIRN

Born: Lower East Side in New York, circa 1900
Excerpts from his published autobiography,
"The Rabbi from Burbank"

Rabbi Isidor Zwirn

Torah is a tree of life to those who take hold of her, Long life is in her hand; In her left hand are riches and honour. Her ways are pleasant ways, and all her paths lead to peace.

The Sabbath began as usual at our Orthodox synagogue until I stepped up to the *bimah,* the platform, to read the weekly portion from the Torah. Then pandemonium broke loose. Before I really knew what was happening, two huge uniformed police officers suddenly appeared, grabbed me by both arms, and started moving me toward the doorway.

"What's happening? What are you doing?" I asked, more startled than angry.

"Just come along quietly, Rabbi," one of the officers said. "We're leaving the synagogue."

"But, why? I belong here. I'm one of the rabbis. I don't understand…"

"Let's go," he said, tightening his grip on my arm.

"But…"

The pressure on my arms increased. "C'mon, Rabbi. Let's go."

I couldn't believe what was happening. For one wild moment I wondered if this was how it had happened in Germany. I looked at the congregants hoping that they would do something, that they would rescue me from these officers. But they just looked at me, most of them with startled looks on their faces. Not a single one of them raised a hand or voice to help me.

Within moments we were off the *bimah*, down the aisle, and out on the street. As soon as the officers released their grip on my arms, I turned to reenter the synagogue. Immediately, they grabbed me again.

"Sorry, Rabbi, but you can't go back in there."

"But I belong in there," I protested. "I'm one of the rabbis…"

One of the huge officers towered above me, shaking his head. "Sorry, Rabbi Zwirn," he said, "but our orders were to remove you from the synagogue, which we did. And to prevent you from entering it, which we're going to do if you try to get back in. Sorry…"

The impact of the officers' words struck me full force: I had just been forcibly ousted from my own synagogue! The action was a harsh reminder to me that, as a Jew, an Orthodox Jew and a rabbi at that, my decision to become a follower of the Messiah was not being looked upon with favour by my fellow Jews.

I came from a long line of Orthodox Jews. Though my father was a tzaddik, a righteous man, he was not a rabbi. Nor was my paternal grandfather of blessed memory, though he was even more strict and pious than my father.

Orthodox Jewish fathers and their sons usually develop a very close and lasting relationship. My father's and mine was no exception. Some of my earliest memories in New York City are sitting with him while we

134

studied the weekly portion from the Torah and Haftarah (a section from the Book of Prophets).

My father wanted me to become a rabbi, just as his father had wanted him to be. For the past 2,000 years or so, any Orthodox Jew who wanted his son to become a rabbi would send him to a Hebrew school called a *yeshivah*, also called, *"house of research."* [57]

From the very first day in the *yeshivah,* our textbook was the Torah. And, of course, the Torah was in Hebrew. As each student was called upon in turn, he had to read the entire sentence and give his interpretation of what the verse meant to him. The teaching rabbi would then give his and other rabbis' interpretation of that verse, and encourage all the students to participate in the ensuing dialogue.

Often this dialogue would center around the meaning of a single word in the sentence. Sometimes the meaning of the entire passage would even hinge upon a single letter of a single word. The discussions that grew out of such intense studies gave rise to the standing joke that whenever two Jews meet for a conversation, you can expect at least three or four different opinions.

Basically, that is how we studied, both in the *yeshivah* and in our homes. This method taught us love and respect for the honest opinions of others, even though they might differ or conflict with our own.

Our learning was accompanied by a catchy tune, that no *yeshivah* child could ever forget, with the words going something like, "And so said Rabbi X…and so said Rabbi Y…and so said Rabbi Z…" and so on.

We were taught, and I firmly believe it to be true, that there is no way of ever arriving at eternal truths unless all concepts and all opinions are allowed to be discussed openly. We were taught that this was the way

---

[57] *Note.* From "The Rabbi from Burbank," by Isidor Zwirn and Bob Owen, 1986, p. 15-16. Copyright 1986 by Kenneth Copeland Publications. Reprinted with permission.

that free men and children of the free were to study life. It could be said that this *bet hamidrash* method of study is based upon the commandment, "Thou shalt love thy neighbor as thyself."

Being a Jewish boy in those days wasn't easy, especially where I lived. Jewish children were often the butt of crude and cruel jokes and even violence. I soon learned to stay away from *goyim*, Gentile boys or men. On more than one occasion they would catch me and treat me shamefully, sometimes burning my face with the glowing end of a cigarette. As I writhed and cried out in pain, they laughed and made slurring remarks about Jews. The first time they called me a "Christ killer," I asked my father about it.[49]

He shook his head, "No, son, we are no more Christ killers than they are. The Romans crucified the Gentiles' Jesus, not the Jews."

Though Pops, as I always called him, was very careful in his speaking about the *goyim,* I realized that he, too, feared and perhaps even hated them. Most of the Jewish community honestly believed that all Gentiles were "Jew haters" and were to be avoided. Consequently, neither my father nor any of our Jewish friends did business with Gentiles if they could help it.

These early experiences solidified my attitudes towards the Gentiles, attitudes which continued throughout my life until recent years. It seemed to me then that Jews and Gentiles had nothing in common. It seemed that the only similarity was that we were both human. However, even at that point the Gentiles seemed to have some doubts about us, as they often called us "swine" and accused us of having horns on our heads like animals.

We dressed differently. We ate differently. Even our schools were different. So, from my earliest childhood and youth, I was led to believe

---

[49] *Note.* From "The Rabbi from Burbank," by Isidor Zwirn and Bob Owen, 1986, p. 21-23. Copyright 1986 by Kenneth Copeland Publications. Reprinted with permission.

that Jews and Gentiles had nothing in common, and we Jews were to have nothing to do with "them."

As a Jewish boy and young man, my every awareness was of Adonai. My thoughts were constantly centered upon the fact of his presence in my life. In the truest sense of the word, it was not just faith in his presence, but distinctly more than that. His presence was a foregone conclusion. I was aware of the *fact* of his presence.

This belief was the result of the prayers that my father taught me to pray when I awakened, before eating or drinking, and upon seeing God's wonders in the universe. Every thought and every action was inextricably connected with God's presence.

The same awareness of Adonai was present in my *bet hamidrash* method of study and learning. I was taught that Adonai not only cared about my learning, but that he commanded me to study and learn Torah, and the accepted method of so doing was through *bet hamidrash.*

To this day, I can hear the voices of my rabbis and teachers as they expounded. "Remember," they said over and over again, "Torah is our textbook. Only Torah. When we study Torah it is both our text and our commentary."[58]

The power of Torah, God's immutable Word, was the center and source of all that we did. As Jewish families, we studied Torah, we lived by Torah, we talked Torah. Our lives were intimately impacted by Torah. The way we lived, the way we died, the way we worshipped, the way we married and treated our wives and children, the way we conducted business—everything we did was a reflection of our Torah. Everything.

---

[58] *Note.* From "The Rabbi from Burbank," by Isidor Zwirn and Bob Owen, 1986, p. 17-18. Copyright 1986 by Kenneth Copeland Publications. Reprinted with permission.

When I was fifteen years old, Pops bought a house in the Bronx, and we moved there from the Lower East Side.[59] After four years I became so knowledgeable about the fur industry that I opened my own shop. Business was good, and I soon went into partnership with two well-established furriers.

I was about twenty-four years of age and doing well in business when I met Rae, the woman who was to become my wife. Since both of us had Orthodox backgrounds, we had no religious disagreements and we peaceably began our lives together.

Despite my good intentions, though, after marriage, the grim realities of making a living during those Depression years put a temporary halt to my regular systematic Torah study. As the children came, first a girl, then a boy, the urgent financial demands upon me increased, and survival became my prime concern.

The long hours of pressured work took their toll on me and I contracted asthma. I hung on as long as I could, but the harsh winters in New York soon proved too much for me.

So I settled business matters and moved my wife, my two children, and myself to Burbank, California.[60] At that time the membership (at Emunah Orthodox Synagogue in Burbank) was very small, hardly a minyan. But shortly after I came, Dr. Bau arrived with his brother-in-law and two other families. This provided us with a strong *minyan* every Sabbath. The congregation learned of my interest in preparing young people for their bar and bat mitzvahs, so they made me responsible for their training. I accepted the opportunity with gusto.

The year was 1950, and by then the Jewish State had been established and interest in Zionism was flourishing. Personally, I had always been

---

[59] *Note.* From "The Rabbi from Burbank," by Isidor Zwirn and Bob Owen, 1986, p. 34-35. Copyright 1986 by Kenneth Copeland Publications. Reprinted with permission.
[60] *Note.* From "The Rabbi from Burbank," by Isidor Zwirn and Bob Owen, 1986, p. 38-39. Copyright 1986 by Kenneth Copeland Publications. Reprinted with permission.

fascinated with prophecies about biblical Zionism and had occasionally thought I would like to study it.

One day Dr. Bau approached me with an interesting question. "Isidor, I understand you are quite interested in Zionism?"

"Very much so."

"Well, I have been reading of a synagogue that appointed one of their men as Rabbi of Zionism. And I think we should have one in our synagogue."

I agreed.

"Will you become our Rabbi of Zionism?"

"Gladly."

Shortly after that conversation, I appeared before the board and was given the official position of Rabbi of Zionism. The declared purpose of this appointment was to research the Scriptures concerning Zionism and then to make my findings known to the congregation.

I lost no time plunging into the subject.[61]

To my astonishment, I found that practically every prophecy in which the word Zion was used was in some way connected with the Messiah. For example, I read, *"For the sake of Zion"* that our Lord *"would not be quiet,"* and *"the Redeemer will come to the Zionists,"* and scores of other such references. Again, as I had before, I wondered why I had never heard these passages discussed publicly.

---

[61] *Note.* From "The Rabbi from Burbank," by Isidor Zwirn and Bob Owen, 1986, p. 43. Copyright 1986 by Kenneth Copeland Publications. Reprinted with permission.

Since satisfactory answers were not immediately forthcoming, I found myself with two choices: I could either forget the whole matter or I could seek out answers for myself. I decided on the latter.

I knew that the *goyim*, the Gentiles, accepted the Messiahship of Yeshua, whom they called Jesus, by faith, which was beyond my comprehension. Of course, I had heard about this Jesus, but I knew little about him. I knew that he was a Jew and that he was a rabbi. I, as any Jew, could easily accept those facts concerning him. But, according to the rumors I had heard about this Jesus, he had been crucified because he had claimed to be God. I took little stock in the claims Yeshua had reportedly made of himself, including his filial relationship with Adonai.

Only incidentally did this Yeshua enter the picture at all. I was researching Zionism. If the study of Zionism were to somehow point to asking questions about the Gentiles' Messiah, well and good. But if not, that was also good.

At any rate, having little certainty as to where my project would take me, I felt a certain excitement as I set out. I believed that I could be relatively objective. No Christian had ever discussed the subject of Yeshua with me. No Christian had ever presented me with his views, nor attempted to "convert" me to his church or to his belief. I was not sick or terminally ill. Nor was I faced with some catastrophic tragedy. I was well and in my right mind. No emotional motive or need impelled me.

I was well aware that no Orthodox rabbi would deny that there is to be a Messiah and a Messianic Age of Zionism. As Zionist Rabbi, my responsibility was to check every single prophecy that had to do with the coming Messiah. Each jot and tittle would have to be examined for one hundred percent accuracy. I, Rabbi Isidor Zwirn, would conduct my study with integrity. I would take the prophecies one at a time, research each one thoroughly, then summarize my conclusions.[62]

For months I systematically examined each of the prophecies. I checked and rechecked them carefully, tabulated each new piece of information that came to light. My notebooks began to bulge with facts, and my mind began to stagger with new possibilities.

I knew that God had provided us with a twofold test by which to check the veracity of a prophet's words. If a prophet's work passed this two-pronged test, he was considered to be a true and faithful prophet. Conversely, if his work did not stand up to this scrutiny, he was clearly not a prophet, but was some sort of charlatan.

First, did this person's prophetic utterances come to pass? Second, would his words stand the test of time? Would they be studied? Would they apply to another century as they applied at the time they were first uttered?

I applied these two tests to each of the prophecies dealing with Zionism and the Jews' Messiah. Then, one by one, I sorted and selected the ones that passed.

It would take a very large book to detail my total investigation of the Zionist Scriptures and to give an exposition of each of the prophecies I researched. Logically, I chose Isaiah as the first and possibly the primary book of the Bible for my investigation.[63]

Having mined the rich ore field of Isaiah, I moved on to the second and third of the three major Zionist Scriptures, Jeremiah 31 and Psalm 110. Each claimed my attention for a different reason.

---

[62] *Note.* From "The Rabbi from Burbank," by Isidor Zwirn and Bob Owen, 1986, p. 58. Copyright 1986 by Kenneth Copeland Publications. Reprinted with permission.
[63] *Note.* From "The Rabbi from Burbank," by Isidor Zwirn and Bob Owen, 1986, p. 63. Copyright 1986 by Kenneth Copeland Publications. Reprinted with permission.

Finally, as does any researcher after truth, whether scientist, logician, or theologian, I reached the point where any more effort would have resulted in diminishing returns. I needed to sift and analyze the facts. I opened my bulging notebooks and carefully examined my notes again. They were well in order. My logic was impeccable. All that remained was for me to compile the results.

I drew a deep breath and reached for my pen. I wrote: **"Every single prophecy that I have researched concerning the coming of Messiah is true, and has come to pass** *exactly as predicted* **by the prophets of Israel."**

I recognized and acknowledged the simple, yet (for me) earth-shattering fact that the Messiah I so long had awaited *had already come*. He had come to earth nearly 2,000 years ago. He had come "unto his own, and his own had received him not." And the name of that divine Person whom I had so painstakingly sought and found in the pages of Torah was he, Yeshua ha Mashiach, Jesus Christ the Messiah: the Messiah of all mankind, *including the Jews*! Including Rabbi Isidor Zwirn.[64]

I had been so immersed in my research that I gave little thought to how my family might respond when I told them what I had been doing and the conclusions I had drawn. But I clearly recall what happened when I broached the subject to them. I didn't make a big deal of my announcement, I just told them, "I have come to the conclusion that the *Yeshua* of the Christians is also the Messiah of the Jews..."

Looking back now, I doubt that I could have said anything that could have shocked them more. The reaction I received from them was, in each case, instantaneous. First a long moment of stunned silence, then the outburst. "You converted to Christianity! You've become a Christian! You converted!"

---

[64] *Note.* From "The Rabbi from Burbank," by Isidor Zwirn and Bob Owen, 1986, p. 85. Copyright 1986 by Kenneth Copeland Publications. Reprinted with permission.

"No, I didn't convert. I just said…"

"I heard what you said. You said you're a Christian!"

"No. I didn't say that. Just listen to me."

"I heard what you said. And you said too much already. You said you've converted, that you're now a follower of that…of that Jesus. That's what you said. And I don't want to hear another word about it."

They didn't just pronounce the word Yeshua or Jesus, they spit it out.

As I listened to the incriminations being heaped upon me *by my own family* because of that name, I was at first unbelieving, then shocked, then hurt. "You just don't understand…" I tried to tell them.[65]

I decided to share my knowledge with the senior rabbi of our synagogue. He listened patiently. He didn't try to dissuade me. All he said was, "Just don't talk about that around here."

I agreed, and thought that might be the end of the matter. But I was mistaken. At that time I was taking some classes at a local university. Everyone there knew I was a Jew, which I had never made any bones about; but now I began talking about something that no Jew should talk about. I began telling my classmates that *Yeshua* was the Messiah. It caused an uproar on the campus.

The news of this got back to my synagogue by means of a student who was the son of one of the synagogue men. "Rabbi Zwirn is telling everyone on the campus that Jesus is the Messiah!" he reported to his father. His father reported it to the council. It might have gone no further, had not the Los Angeles Orthodox Jewish Council stepped in.

---

[65] *Note.* From "The Rabbi from Burbank," by Isidor Zwirn and Bob Owen, 1986, p. 90. Copyright 1986 by Kenneth Copeland Publications. Reprinted with permission.

"This is disgraceful," they said. So they did something about it. They sent a communiqué to the council of my synagogue. "Unless Rabbi Zwirn is physically prevented from participating in synagogue services, we will cease to recognize the orthodoxy of your synagogue."

That did it. The following Sabbath as I stepped up to the *bimah* to participate in the service, two burly policemen appeared, ushered me out of the synagogue, and ordered me to stay out.

Thinking back, even though I was and will always remain a Jew, I should have anticipated my fellow Jews' reaction. I realized that I was naively unprepared for the explosive reception that resulted from my announcement that I, Orthodox Rabbi Isidor Zwirn, now believed that the feared and hated Jesus of the Christians was actually the Jews' long-awaited Messiah, and that he was indeed, *Yeshua ha Mashiach,* Jesus the Messiah.[66]

I did learn that anyone, Jew or Greek (Gentile or Barbarian), can come to know Adonai our Messiah through the Spirit of Truth. I learned that anyone who researched him with integrity in the same manner in which he researched our Father *Adonai* and Holy Spirit *Elohim*, the fullness *(echad)* of the One Living God can be found.

Our Father guarantees it. *"And ye shall seek me, and find me, when ye shall search (doresh) for me with all your heart. And I will be found of you, saith Adonai"* *(*Jeremiah 29:13-14).[67]

כי לו האמנתם במשה האמנתם גם בי כי עלי הוא כתב

For if you believed Moses, you would believe Me;

for he wrote about Me.

John 5:46 יוחנן